Spared Angola

Memories From A Cuban-American Childhood

By

Virgil Suárez

Arte Público Press
Houston, Texas
1997

This volume is made possible through grants from the National Endowment for the Arts (a federal agency), the Andrew W. Mellon Foundation, The Cultural Arts Council of Houston and the Lila Wallace Reader's Digest Fund.

Recovering the past, creating the future

Arte Público Press
University of Houston
Houston, Texas 77204-2090

Cover design by Susan Barber

Suárez, Virgil.
   Spared Angola: Memories from a Cuban-American Childhood, /by Virgil Suárez
      p.   cm.
   ISBN 1-55885-197-6 (alk. paper)
   I. Cuban-Americans—Literary collections. 2. Cuban-Americans—Social Life and Customs. I. Title.
   PS3569.U18S63   1997
   813—dc21   96-39825
                                                    CIP

Acknowledgments

The author thanks the following literary magazines and their editors in which some of these poems have appeared: *New Delta Review, The Exquisite Corpse, Colorado Review, The American Voice, Sundog: The Southeast Review, Apalachee Quarterly, Latino Stuff Review, The Americas Review, Many Mountains Moving, Puerto del Sol, Rio Grande Review, Borderlands: Texas Poetry Review, International Poetry Review, Prairie Schooner, The Southern Review, The Massachusetts Review, SLANT: Journal of Poetry and Ideas, The Caribbean Review, Blue Mesa Review, Forkroads, Cimarron* and *Multicultural Review.*

"Flash Flesh" in *Under The Pomegranate Tree: Latino Erotica*, edited by Ray González, published by Pocket Books, Simon and Schuster, 1996.

"Bitterness" reprinted in *Muy Macho*, an anthology of Latino mens' essays, edited by Ray González, published by Anchor/Doubleday, 1997.

I would also like to thank my wife, Delia Poey, for her devotion and meticulous proofing of the text. For encouragement and heartfelt editing, my publisher and guardian angel, Nicolás Kanellos. Many thanks to the Arte Público Press family for the good work. I am indebted for their support and inspiration to the following poets: Agha Shahid Ali, Gustavo Perez-Firmat, Ricardo Pau-Llosa, Leroy V. Quintana, Victor Hernández Cruz, Quincy Troupe, Carolina Hospital, Pablo Medina, Juan Felipe Herrera, Francisco Alarcón, Andrei Codrescu, David Kirby, Barbara Hamby, Alberto Ríos, Judith Ortiz Cofer, Martín Espada, Tino Villanueva, Ray González and Wasabi Kanastoga.

Books By Virgil Suárez

The Cutter (novel)

Latin Jazz (novel)

Welcome to The Oasis (novella & stories)

Havana Thursdays (novel)

Going Under (novel)

Iguana Dreams: New Latino Fiction (as co-editor, anthology)

Paper Dance: 55 Latino Poets (as co-editor, anthology)

*Little Havana Blues: A Contemporary Cuban-American
Literature Anthology* (as co-editor)

Contents

For my parents with respect and admiration
And Wasabi Kanastoga, blood brother

Tin marín de los pingüé,
Cúcara mácara títere fue.

Spared Angola

After a twenty-year absence, my grandmother, Donatila, flies from Havana to Miami for a visit. Waiting for her in the crowded and noisy lobby of Miami International Airport, I am struck by memories of my childhood in the arms of this woman who, except for vague moments, is a perfect stranger. To my mother she is Tina of the constant aches and headaches, of the bouts with rheumatism, of the skin disease that spotted her face and neck with pink blotches, of the hair the color of smoke and straw. *Abuela* Tina. Twenty years before this moment caught in the restless humdrum of waiting, this woman about to visit showed me many things: how to feed leftover rice to chickens, tie my shoelaces, brew the kind of watery coffee I like to drink with toasted bread. She kept my behind from feeling the wrath of my father's belt on numerous occasions; she stayed with me while I took a shower in the room by the side of the clapboard house because I was terrified of the bullfrogs that sought the humidity trapped there. She told me stories, most of which I've forgotten, except for the one about the old hag who would wait for a man to come by on horseback to cross the old bridge. The hag would jump on the horse and spook the animal and the rider. The horsemen knew never to look back or risk spooking themselves crazy. "Never look back," she said, "as you cross your bridges." The flight arrives and the waiting intensifies. My mother sinks her nails into my flesh as she holds my hand. My father every so often retrieves a handkerchief from his back pocket (he's never used one) and wipes his forehead and under his eyes. The first few passengers come out the glass doors of Customs and are greeted by relatives who have never forgotten these tired and worn faces, frail bodies. Parents, sisters, brothers, sons, daughters, all now looking thirty-six years older. "Time," my father says, "is a son of a bitch." Finally, I spot my aunt (I have not seen her for as long as I have not seen my grandmother), my father's sister who'd gotten cancer. She is holding on to my grandmother, and I realize my memory has served me better than I am willing to admit. Grandmother Tina looks the same except for the patches of the skin disease which have completely taken over her face. My mother screams and lets go of my hand and runs to the arms of her mother. My father to his sister. I stand back and brace myself. After the hugs and the kisses, my mother says, "There he is! Your grandson, Mamá!" She walks toward me and I find I cannot move, for I cannot believe in movement; I am still stuck in time. She comes toward me. *"¿No te acuerdas de mí?"* she says, her Spanish the necessary tug. I lean into her arms, for she is small and frail, and we stand there in the middle of the lobby. I tell her that I do remember. I remember everything. Slowly now we make our way out of the terminal to the parking lot, into the car, onto the freeway, home to my parents', up the stairs and into the living room of an apartment in which I've spent so very little time. All this time everybody has been talking except me; I've been driving and listening, bewildered by all the catching up. In the living room now, waiting for refreshments, my grandmother comes over to where I sit and she holds my face between her hands.

🕎 *Virgil Suárez*

She looks into my eyes. Can I? Can I remember this woman? My grandmother Donatila. She's an apparition, I think, but don't say it. She says, "You must tell me about you, all that the distance has taken from us." I tell her I am happy to see her, after so much time. *"¿Sabes?"* she says. "You are a lucky young man. Your parents did the right thing. When they took you out of Cuba, your parents spared you. Yes, you were spared. Spared Angola."

Donatilia's Unrequited
Love Remedy

a brewed *tacita* of espresso
dark & bitter
some crushed leaves
of *yerba buena*
cobwebs
plucked from a vacant room
pillow hair (from the subject)
& one whole *colibrí*
feathers & all
stir over intense fire
bring to a boil
let simmer
once cooled
the trick then is to get
the person to drink it

Virgil Suárez

Teresa *La Pasamanos*

whom my mother took me
to whenever I ate too much candy
or nuts & I became *empachado*.
Teresa, in the light of the candles
during Havana city blackouts
soothed my aching belly
with silken hands as she gently
rubbed oil & anointed *pomadas*
against my skin & made everything
right again! Where are you?
Where are you now after so much
time & distance? Teresa,
healer of my youth.

Sapos/Bullfrogs

before the days of fear
    they entered *Tía* Silvia's house
        through holes in the walls
hid in least expected places
    lived in cold crevices
        in the middle of the night
they knocked down objects
    silenced crickets in their wake
        croakedcroakedcroaked
to announce the downpours
    best mosquito control said my aunt
        countless lived in the house
undisturbed they came & went like family
    in a luckless country
        they brought good fortune

Virgil Suárez

What Was Done to Turn Bulls into Oxen

for Reinaldo Arenas, after "Violence"
from his book *Before Night Falls*

I too witnessed the violence as a child.

The tied-up bull raged & kicked
But the *güajiros* held it steady.

They took its testicles, placed them
On an anvil & with a wood mallet

Smashed them to a pulp. With the first
Blow the bull let out a fierce, horrible

Shriek, its nostrils flaring, its eyes gone
White to the world, saliva frothing

In its mouth. The beast trembled
& its front legs buckled in surrender

Under its weight & the blows kept
Falling. Between repulsion & fascination,

I stood there, hands balled up into fists,
My knuckles gone pale, choked by a scream

by what was done to that mean
& wild bull that one afternoon.

La Ceiba: Tree of Life

We children played within the folds of its elephant-skin roots, lost to the outside world, no politics here, no parents, only us and the sounds of our pleasure howls. Here we lowered our pants and showed our penises to each other—none of us had the right size, for how could we at such an age? We peed against the tree trunk and watched as the urine ran down the trunk to disappear into the reddish dirt. We carved our names on the roots of this tree, along with the names of the girls we didn't yet like but whose names we knew and carved anyway. We played cowboys and Indians, hide-and-seek, and sometimes we gathered the *centavos* left as *brujería* offerings to *Las Siete Potencias*. Of course we didn't know about respect then, so we disturbed the amulet offerings. Sometimes, we found a dead chicken or a white dove, feathers gone ashen with the stain of dirt and tainted by spilled blood. This, of course, scared us and we ran away. Sometimes though, we stayed and watched as the ants helped with decomposition as they carried bits and pieces in relay lines off to a nearby underground nest. So many mornings and afternoons we lived here, undisturbed, isolated, until the one day when lightning hit the tree and it died. Then we slowly became victims of our own mischief and undoing. Aimless became a new word in our vocabulary.

The Dirt Eaters

Whenever we grew tired and bored of curb ball,
   of encircling the scorpions we found under rocks

by the mother-in-law tongues within a fiery circle
   of kerosene, and watched as they stung themselves

to death, we ate dirt: soft, grainy, pretend chocolate
   dirt, in our fantasies sent to us by distant relatives

in *El Norte. Fango*. We stood in a circle, wet the dirt
   under our bare feet, worked with our fingers to crumble

the clogs with our nails, removed the undesired twigs,
   pebbles, and beetles. Dirt—how delicious. How filling.

We ate our share of it back then. Beto, the youngest,
   warned us not to eat too much, it could make us sick,

give us the shits, vomit, or even worse, worms.
   We laughed. We ridiculed him. We chanted

after him: *"¡Lo que no mata, engorda!*
   ¡Lo que no mata, engorda!"

What doesn't kill you, makes you fat, and stronger.

Virgil Suárez

Tejedor y su grupo

I remember he came over to Yiya and Gustavo's house, driven over by Talo, the group's driver and guide. Tejedor was blind then and needed to be taken by the hand. He sat in the back yard because inside the house it was always hot. They came here, I suppose, between gigs, to take a long break. They sat in the patio and drank beers. Gustavo and Yiya stayed inside because they didn't like Talo, who was dating Esperanza, Yiya and Gustavo's ex-daughter-in-law. It was a complicated situation, as it continues to be as I look back through the years. But this is not about that; this is about Tejedor, a mulatto music treasure, someone who's left us some wonderful music, not lost, not yet. Our house was next door, so whenever I heard the commotion, I grabbed a chair and pulled myself up over the tall brick wall. There I sat with my legs dangling, then Tejedor would turn to the scraping of my shoes against the wall. He'd say, *"Fiñe, te vas a romper el coco."* I loved the deep, hollow sound of his voice. I loved the way he put words together to create sound. He signaled one of the members of his "Grupo" to catch me and pull me down.

Tejedor wanted always to put his hand on my head. *"Coco duro,"* he'd say, referring to my hard-headedness. Always he brought something for me: a pair of maracas, claves, a *guayo*—over the couple of years that he visited Yiya's and Gustavo's, my collection grew. He even brought me a violin once. It didn't have strings, but I pretended I could play anyway. Sometimes, Tejedor y su Grupo started rehearsing, then he'd let me join in, even if most of the time the only thing I was good for was for making the other players lose their beat. I was beating out my own rhythm, and for this I will forever be thankful to Tejedor. Tejedor, blind, gray-haired, soft around the belly, between *sones* and *boleros,* you became an undemanding muse for a child with nothing to lose and the world to gain.

Virgil Suárez

Manuel & Josefina

There's a picture of the two I keep in my office and which my mother brought back from Cuba, taken by her during her visit there in 1983. Manuel and Josefina, next-door neighbors when we ourselves lived in Havana. The picture shows clearly what time does to the human body, to the human face. They stand there by the wood rocker I knew as a child when I visited on the many afternoons I came to play with their son Ricardito. Manuel, or "Mino" as I called him, sat there and rocked as he listened to the radio—his favorite shows from El Norte: "Sherlock Holmes" and "The Shadow." He sat there and rocked and listened and when the shows were over and silence returned, I could still hear the rocking from the porch where Ricardito and I played with *caracoles* and our string *fuetes*—which were bottle caps we had sharpened and made with strings into hand yo-yo's. Whoever cut the opponents string won. Mino rocked even in his sleep. That's why he loved that rocker, because he said it knew what to do on its own. Josefina worked in the kitchen. She cooked and cleaned, and made the afternoon *café-con-leche*. What I remember most about her was the way she bit her tongue as she cooked, lost in concentration, the steam of her cooking fogging up her thick glasses. She claimed it was the aroma of her cooking that put Manuel to sleep so quickly. He rocked, she cooked. Sometimes too he taught me how to roll cigars. He rolled them and sold them on the block. I never did ask what kind of work Manuel did for a living, but whatever it was allowed him to come home in the afternoons to eat lunch, rock and listen to the radio, and have an afternoon *cafecito*. I visited and played with their son. So the days went and the years. And when my parents left and took me out of the country, we gave everything we owned to Manuel and Josefina. My mother said that they still had everything, including the broken television. But in the picture all that is captured is Mino (in his V-neck undershirt) and Josefina with a smile and a squint in her eyes behind her thick-framed, bottle-bottom glasses. This is the way my mother captured them. Mino, who hit me for the very first time because I talked back to him, said some awful things like *me cago en ti* or *maricón* or *hijo de puta*, for what I cannot recall. Josefina, who collected leaves and preserved them between the pages of her cookbooks. They died within two weeks of each other: Mino in his rocking chair and Josefina in bed, found several days later by Ricardo (no longer Ricardito, for he, like so many of us, had grown up). My mother didn't tell me news of their passing until years later for fear that it, the bad news, as she always called people dying, would affect me in a hard way. Well, no getting around that, especially since I now have their photograph hung in my office. Every day I come to work I look at it and remember—that's all we are here to do now.

Virgil Suárez

Scenes from an Otherwise
Normal Childhood

Ask somebody. Anybody. Ask a dentist, a mechanic, a plumber, an electrician, a bricklayer, a lawyer, a doctor, a priest. A bartender who'll tell you he's heard it a million times. Go ahead, ask a man about to cross the street. An athlete, an artist, a masseuse. Ask the man standing on the ledge of a fifth-floor tenement window. Ask the presidents, the dictators, the ambassadors, the congressmen and senators, ask the judges. Yes, ask the judges and members of a hung jury. Ask them, and they will all tell you that there comes a time in a man's life when he must confront his past, stare at it eye-to-eye, have a showdown. Because the longer he waits, the more aimless and rootless his life becomes. You climb to the misty peak of a mountain from where you can see a valley stretched out in the horizon. See wood houses, a church and its tall steeple, a town, people, animals grazing . . . that is the past. It is, as not only psychologists would agree, all too important. A man must count his chips before he can continue to gamble.

One is born, and from that point on the adventures begin. Whether a man is to suffer or live happily thereafter does not matter. What matters is that someday he will die. This notion, sooner or later, becomes the propeller, the driving force behind men from all walks of life. Some men learn to disguise their fear of dying behind masks of courage, strength, ambition . . .

A childhood, then, is something precious.

The child (as I call myself in order to achieve the necessary distance from which to see clearly) is born on the 29th of January, 1962, in the Sagrado Corazón de Jesús Hospital in old Havana. Five-thirty in the afternoon. It is that time when the heat of the afternoon begins to subside. Imagine the slap on the ass. The upside-down, red-faced baby crying as he breathes his first gulps of air while outside a whole city is coming out of the shade and into the open sea breeze. It is a city on the move. An indifferent city full of noise and commotion.

Three years before the child is born, his father buys the house in Arroyo Naranjo, a little town on the outskirts of the big city. Batista is no longer in power; the father has quit the police force. He works as a pattern cutter in a tailor shop. His being a policeman is never spoken about again.

Arroyo Naranjo is about thirty minutes from Jose Martí Airport in Rancho Boyeros. Arroyo means brook. Naranjo orange. So. The town where he is to live and grow up in is called orange brook, though there isn't a brook that color in the city, or one that cuts through an orange orchard or field. "It is just a name," his father tells him the day the child asks about it. Names are just that. Names.

It is a quiet neighborhood, but the people who populate its homes and streets are odd. There are the Figueroas and Delgados who won't speak to each other because Mister Delgado doesn't mow his lawn regularly. Old Monson's son is still missing (secret police arrested him) and Monson has taken a lover, a man much younger than his son. The Carpios are devout *santeros,* and usually a passerby can find coconuts and dead chickens at the corner of their house where the street light doesn't work. Marcelino, an alcoholic, has just been run over by a bus in downtown Havana. His wife, Mirta, put the house up for sale. Among other men in the neighborhood, Mirta is known for walking naked inside the house. The gasman and mailman have seen her. A branch from the old cieba tree has fallen over Teresa's roof and she doesn't have any money for repairs. When it rains, her living room and kitchen flood. Beside being known for drinking fire water and sleep walking, she is the best *pasamanos,* meaning that people believe she has healing powers in her fingertips. Whenever somebody's child is sick, he or she is taken to see Teresa first, who will then rub a concoction made from oils and herbs over the kid's stomach while she sweats profusely and the sweat trickles down her forehead and nose and mixes with the oils as she rubs. Agustín, the kitemaker, is going blind with cataracts and he will die not wanting to go see a doctor. He claims doctors are quacks. Then there is the Echevarría's abandoned mansion at the corner of Luz Street. People say it is haunted. Echevarría and his family were killed by the Coast Guard as they tried to leave clandestinely. Weeds have taken over the lawns and once-upon-a-time beautiful gardens. El Volcán, the bodega, is managed by a Chinese family. Chan Li, the proprietor, likes to joke about how he took his family out of China to escape communism and now communism has found them in Cuba. "No more running," he says. *"Aquí me quedo."* Here he stays put.

Such is the place when the child, wrapped in a blue blanket, is taken in a taxi from the hospital to the house in Arroyo Naranjo.

At first glance the house looks small, but it isn't. Beige with yellow window trims and awnings, the house stands in the middle of two rows of *palmeras* and papaya trees. Roses of all colors crown the entrance. It rained recently and everything is wet. The happy couple, man with his arm over wife's shoulder, woman holding wrapped baby in her arms, enters through the wrought-iron gates and stand on the Italian-tiled floor of the porch. The floor is either wet or glazed, because it is the shiniest floor.

The man opens the door and the woman and baby enter. Everything inside the house smells clean, as if brand new. The living room furniture, the T.V., the radio. Between the living room and dining room sits a thirty-gallon aquarium with all kinds of colorful fish in it. Suddenly, when they enter, the fish stop swimming. Open mouthed and wide eyed, they float like leaves fallen in a pond.

Although the baby's eyes are not open, the mother takes him over to the aquarium for a closer look. In it are fat, veil-tailed, red and black, white and red gold fish. Their faces look deformed because of their masks of bulging skin. These fish will still be there by the time the child grows older. Whether they are the same ones or not, he'll never know. Maybe they reproduce or his father goes out to a pet shop and keeps buying new ones. They are magical, though, and the mere act of looking at them consumes hours of the boy's childhood.

From the living room the mother takes him to the smallest room in the house. His room! Its walls are covered with wood cutouts of cartoon characters. Woody Woodpecker. Snow White and all but one of the Seven Dwarfs. (He can't remember which one was missing, though he always imagines Sneezy to have died of pneumonia.) The next-door neighbors' kid has died of pneumonia. There is also Chilly Willy and Casper, the friendly ghost, adorning a wall. On the inside of the crib are rubber and stuffed toys and a wind-up mobile that plays "Raindrops Keep Falling on My Head" as ducklings, hanging from their strings and wires, follow the mama and papa ducks. A Pinocchio marionette, arms and legs bent awk-

🐢   Virgil Suárez

wardly, hangs from the ceiling in the corner of the room. The child believes Pinocchio's nose grows very long at night.

The child's room is the sunniest and brightest room in the house, and it seems like he spends an eternity there, playing with his toes, sucking on his fingers and chanting goos and gaas. It is there that the world seems at its best: colorful, warm and caring.

The rest of the house he sees at night when the mother breast-feeds him as she walks back and forth, from her bedroom to the kitchen, from the kitchen to the bathroom and from there back to the bedroom. He learns later that some women have to walk while breast-feeding because the baby suckling at their nipples hurts them. It is only a way to forget about the pain.

The rooms are decorated with dark, heavy oak furniture, which hurts the child when he bangs his head or elbows or knees against it. The parents' bed is so big it looks like an ocean of mattress and sheets and pillows.

Pictures of other members of the family hang from the walls. Porcelain figurines (which he will break and for which he'll get a good spanking) of ballerinas and clowns stand on the mother's mirrored dresser. One of the ballerinas dances around when somebody winds the box on which she tiptoes. The child wonders if people, too, in order to function have to be wound up.

Some are.

Days go by quickly after the child begins to walk. To talk. At first his steps are wobbly, unsure. He holds on to things, and when there isn't anything to hold on to he falls, using his behind as a cushion. (Padded cloth diapers.) His words, too, don't come out straight. A lot of guttural, throaty noises. Screams. But then words form: *"¡Papá!" "¡Mamá!"*

The child evolves into a boy.

The parents are proud. They teach their son how to clap his hands and sing nursery rhymes. During the daily bath in the late afternoon, the father sings to him, *"María Caracoles baila el Mozambique!"* Afterward, the father plays with the boy in the room. Every day he brings the boy a new toy. To the boy he seems so tall, gigantic, unreachable. Only when the father picks him up is the boy able to look at his father's big brown eyes. The way the father's flesh wrinkles around his eyes when he smiles is fascinating.

The father at twenty-nine is thin but muscular, his muscles bulging under his clothes. When the boy grows up he wants to be just like his father. Quick, steady hands never seem to let go, to make a mistake and let the boy fall. Some days his father dresses in suits, neck button undone and loosened necktie around his neck. Tropical weather's too hot for ties. Another thing to grab hold of. The father's cologne makes the boy sneeze. He doesn't like the strong, choking smell.

When the father smokes he tries not to be around the boy, usually doing so in the living room while reading the newspaper. The boy has heard his father coughing late at night and imagines a dragon has snuck inside the house while everyone sleeps.

The boy spends most of his afternoons in a playpen in the living room while his mother works in the kitchen, rattling pots and pans. She talks to him as if he understands.

"So many things, God," she says, peeling yuca and potatoes over the sink. "She's retired now. Needs a place to go."

She is talking about her mother-in-law coming to live with them.

The mother works quickly as she cuts, slices, shreds, prepares all the condiments for the soup she is making. A potent onion-and-garlic aroma reaches the boy in the living room. His eyes water. He cries.

Connections are a wonderful thing. When he cries he knows somebody will come to the rescue, to find out what is wrong. His mother picks him up and out of the playpen. She holds him with cold, wet hands. Wrapping his short arms around his mother's neck, he puts his cheek to hers. She kisses him.

Virgil Suárez

Then the grandmother comes to live in the house. Like his father, she is tall and strongly built. She is a very happy person and shows it in her outgoing personality, her life's-too-short-not-to-have-fun attitude. She and her daughter-in-law get along very well. Something the father appreciates. The boy likes his grandmother because now he's got more people around with whom to play. His grandmother—he calls her Mima—is terrific. She knows how to make bread out of playdough, and people and animals and things . . . she cuts and glues paper-link chains and decorates herself and the boy with them. She's so wonderful.

During siesta in the afternoon, the boy likes to nap with his grandmother, then wake up next to her and tickle her ear-lobes. Comb her ashen hair. Mima lets him get away with everything. She even lets him stick his fingers in her mouth and touch her teeth. She sticks her tongue out at him. This makes him giggle with pleasure.

"Who's the greatest Mima on this big island?" she asks the boy.

"You," says the boy.

"And who's the most beautiful child on the face of this planet?"

The boy knows the answer by now, but, playing dumb, doesn't say anything. He's familiar with the outcome. His grandmother tickles him until he gives her the answer.

"Me!" he says.

"And who do you love most in the whole wide world?"

"Mima."

"Show me how much."

The boy stretches his arms out as far as he can. This makes the grandmother laugh so hard that she begins to cough. She coughs uncontrollably, her face turning red.

Eventually she comes to. She goes to the kitchen to drink water. Everywhere the grandmother goes, the boy follows her. Sometimes she lets him ride on her foot as he holds on to her legs.

"You should have that cough checked," the boy's mother says.

"It's nothing," Mima says. Her voice is like a melody. "It's my asthma."

Asthma. This is the first word whose sound the boy learns to love, though he pronounces it with a lisp. *Asthma!* What a mysterious word.

At night they eat together. His parents, Mima, and the boy sitting on a high chair. The conversations are of an adult matter, topics that he can't and won't understand until years later. The situation of the country is changing. Some sort of census has been taken to establish what will be known as the *libreta* or ration book, something everyone will have to use in order to buy food and clothes. The father doesn't like what's going on. He says the country is turning communist. Should they leave the country? he asks, but nobody answers him. His is an idea that has been kicking around in his head for a while. The question of possibly having to leave her parents, sisters and brothers behind is a disturbing one to the mother. She has no immediate answers.

In the midst of a childhood, moments seem to be ephemeral in a very wonderful, now-you-see-it-now-you-don't sort of way. They are fluid, and now the boy finds himself in the province of Las Villas, in a town called San Pablo, at his maternal grandparent's house. It is summer and the wood house is full of voices and smells. There is a party in progress. The whole family has gathered.

The grandfather, a gray haired man of fifty-two, sits at the head of the table, behind the corn fritters and fried plantain platters, whose steam rises and makes the old man lick his lips. He is discussing with his sons and daughters how much land and cattle the government has taken away. Most of the land is being used for sugar cane. Needless to say, he doesn't like what's going on. But it's his land, godamn it, and they can't take it away from him.

Virgil Suárez

"Sure they can," says the boy's father, who is sitting to the old man's right hand.

The old man's face grows stern, then he says, "You don't know what you're talking about. This was my great grandfather's land, and my grandfather's, and my father's and now mine."

To appease both men, the grandmother who has a strange skin disease which has bleached her skin into pink blotches and spots, puts her bony hand on her husband's shoulder and says, "Isn't it nice, Domingo, that the family is all here?"

Everyone seems anxious to start eating. One of the boy's uncles picks up his fork and knife but suddenly stops when Domingo, his father, looks at him.

The uncle puts the silverware down for he knows that at family gatherings like this one, nobody eats until Domingo says a short prayer.

"Lord," the grandfather begins. "Help us keep the land from which this precious food comes. Don't let those savages take it away from us. Bless our home and family and today's food. Thank you, Lord."

In unison everyone says their amens, then the boy's mother helps her mother and older sister serve the rice, fried pork chunks, boiled cassava with *mojito*, avocado and onion salad, and bread.

The children, who are eating at a separate table, finish before the adults and leave to go outside and play under the big guayaba tree. The guayaba tree stands next to the pig sties. The boys climb the tree and pick green guayabas to throw at the pigs, who, when hit hard enough, squeal.

Most of the boy's cousins are older, more agile and rambunctious. They get bored easily of playing the same game, so when they are through bothering the pigs, the boys wrestle with the girls. The girls pull on each other's hair.

Reina, who is almost ten, five years older than the boy, takes him by the hand and they go for a walk. It is hard for him to walk at her pace. She is a nervous kid with dark droopy eyes and is, of course, a lot bigger and heavier than he is. The boy doesn't know where she's taking him and he doesn't care. She's telling him the story of the witches on the other side of the bridge.

"You know the bridge," she says and tugs at his hand. "Haven't you seen it? It's two miles from here. Where the dried-up canal is. Everybody has to pass it coming or going."

The boy looks up at her. Reina looks nothing like his uncle. Her mother's features dominate her looks and personality. Reina keeps walking and telling him the story.

"Father says kids shouldn't be on the other side of the bridge when the sun goes down. You know why?"

The boy shrugs.

"Because the witches will find you and they'll throw you in this big pot of boiling pig's fat and cook you until you turn soggy." This is the story Donatila has told the children before.

She pauses here and looks at the boy. She turns in the direction of the house. Beads of sweat have formed on her upper lip and nose. Reina will grow up to be a hardnosed communist. She will go to school where she will learn Russian and be awarded a scholarship to travel to the Soviet Union to specialize in the language, and upon her return she will meet and marry a young, high-ranking officer in the Air Force.

"So the witches will dance naked around the pot," she says as they go all the way around to the back of the latrines. "You don't believe me, huh?"

"I believe you," the boy says, feeling a bit confused as to what it is Reina is up to.

"Well, it's true."

She takes him inside one of the two latrines and closes the door behind them. Inside, the latrine is dark, but they can see because of the sunlight that sneaks in through the cracks in the roof. A smell of rotting wood and mildew fills the boy's lungs. Reina and he barely fit in such a small place.

"Promise not to tell," Reina says, "if I let you touch me?"

🕸 *Virgil Suárez*

The boy doesn't want to touch her. His cousin takes his hand and puts it in the inside of her blouse. Her skin feels sticky. She touches him, too, inside his pants.

"Squeeze it," she says a little out of breath.

The boy doesn't want any trouble, and besides he doesn't know what he is doing, so he does what Reina says.

"Put your finger here," she says, taking his hand and placing it between her legs.

That part of her body is sweaty. The boy thinks he smells her pee. That he doesn't like, so he takes his hand away.

"Aw, come on, leave it. Don't stop."

"We better go," says the boy.

"Nobody knows where we are."

She lowers his pants and fondles his peepee. When she squeezes one of his testicles, he jerks back. "Ow! That hurts."

Reina doesn't say anything. She's concentrating, it seems, on whatever it is that she's doing. On her knees, she begins to kiss it. She puts all of it in her mouth, and for a minute the boy wonders if she will bite it off and eat it.

It's getting hot inside the latrine and the smell is getting worse. The mosquitoes are starting to bite him. Reina pulls him down on top of her and wraps her legs around his waist. Her elbows and knees knock against the rotting wood of the latrine, and the sounds remind him of horse hooves going thud-thud! Thud-thud! She squeezes him against her. Between her legs he is lost. He is so nervous and uncomfortable that on her next squeeze he pees all over her.

She stands quickly as if he's dropped a block of ice down her back. He closes his eyes and finishes urinating. It feels good to relieve his bladder.

"Dummy," Reina says. "What did you do that for?"

The pee disappears through the cracks on the floor boards.

"Look what you've done to my skirt," she says.

The boy wants to say he's sorry, but he just looks at her.

"My mother'll want to know what happened," she says, looking down at how the circle widens as the urine is absorbed by the material of her skirt. Then she opens the latrine door and exits, leaving him behind with his pants around his ankles.

About the incident with Reina he doesn't say anything. He tries to keep it a secret, one of those memories better left alone, untouched. But for some reason a year later he tells his cousin Jaime, who has come to live with them for a while in Havana. They are trying to sleep but the mosquitoes which have snuck inside the net and the heat won't let them. The boy's uncle and aunt have sent Jaime to Havana—and this the boy will not know about until years later—to see a psychiatrist.

Jaime claims that when he goes inside a church Saints and Virgins speak to him. He has conversations with the statuettes. What they talk to him about he won't say. At first, of the conversations, his parents think they mean Jaime has a lot of faith. He talks to the figures and bas-reliefs the way a normal child talks to an imaginary friend. But they change their minds when all Jaime talks about is of becoming a priest. He hears the calling. To Jaime, being an only child has been hard, especially not having somebody around to play with.

The boy's parents are in charge of taking Jaime twice a month to see the psychiatrist in Havana. They leave the boy with Mima.

Anyway, they are trying to go to sleep that night when Jaime, after praying, starts to talk about sins. How kids shouldn't do anything bad. He speaks in general terms, which throws a blanket of doubt and confusion over the boy. Has he, the boy, ever done anything he regrets or might regret later on?

It is then that he tells his cousin about what he did—or rather, what Reina made him do inside the latrine.

🌸   Virgil Suárez

Jaime sits up on the bed and begins to act real nervous, jittery. "Oh, God," he says. "They are not liking it . . . what you have just said."

"Who is 'they?'" the boy asks.

"Your guardian angels," says Jaime.

The boy is surprised. He didn't know he had more than one, at least not in the room with him. "Tell me about them," the boy says.

"They are upset with you," Jaime says.

"It wasn't my fault."

"You have to repent."

"What do I have to do?"

"Tell your parents they must take us to church. I will talk to Judas Tadeo personally."

"Judas Tadeo?"

"You don't know who that is?" Jaime asks. "He's the Patron Saint of the Impossible."

The boy feels lost now, knowing that he has upset one of the saints. He shouldn't have told Jaime anything about Reina. He should have kept it a secret. But wouldn't that be cheating the saints? No wonder they are mad at him. He's been a liar.

"Okay," the boy tells his cousin. "I will tell my father to take us to church."

"If you don't," Jaime says, letting his hand fall on the boy's head, "you might be in more trouble than I might be able to talk you out of."

That night the boy has terrible dreams and wakes up sweating. The sheets feel damp. Of course, they are damp because Jaime has peed all over them in his sleep. He can't understand why Jaime, two years older than him, still pees in bed.

In the light of morning, the boy gets a closer look at his cousin's face. There are freckles under Jaime's eyes and on his nose. His skin is pale. It reminds the boy of milk. From the corner of Jaime's mouth hangs dry spittle; and sleep crusties are around the sealed eyes. It is then that the boy realizes that his cousin is, not because of being older or taller or anything like that, a stranger. A very strange stranger.

When the boy's mother finds out the sheets are wet, the boy decides to take the blame, because he is embarrassed for his cousin. Don't do it again is what his mother tells him as she leads him to the bathroom to give him a bath.

"Will you take me to church?" the boy asks his mother.

The mother looks at her son with a gleam of surprise in her eyes. "Why do you want to go to church?"

"I want to see Jaime talk to the saints."

"You believe he can?" the mother asks as she removes the boy's wet pajama pants.

"Maybe they do talk to him," the boy says, stepping into the tub.

The mother decides to tell her son the truth. "Your cousin is disturbed. He has dillusions."

"What are dillusions?"

"He believes he can talk to inanimate objects."

"What are inanimate objects?"

"The word's *in-ani-mate*. Things."

"But saints are not things."

"No, they aren't, but humans can't have conversations with a statue."

"Is it possible to have more than one guardian angel?"

"Sure."

"Jaime says I have many."

"It's possible."

"And I can talk to them."

"All you can do is pray at night; your guardian angel will listen."

The shampoo gets in the boys eyes and it stings. The mother throws water on the boy's face. She is concerned about Jaime talking nonsense to her son. Perhaps she will have the boy's cousin sleep in a separate room. Maybe in Mima's room on the spring-sprung bed.

Virgil Suárez

"If Jaime tells you anything you don't understand, you come to me, all right? I'll clarify whatever confuses you."

"Yes, *Mamá*."

He wonders what she might have to say if he told her about Reina. But he doesn't want to make a mistake and upset his mother, so he decides that from now on he will keep the incident what it is meant to be: a secret.

Talo & the Coupe de Ville

As driver for Tejedor Y Su Grupo, Talo made a steady living. It was being on the road that attracted him to driving as work. That and the fact that he loved his car. I remember the glint on the chrome, the shine and smoothness of the leather interior. He let me climb inside and pretend I was driving. The radio worked so we listened to music. Sometimes he let me help him wash the car. Not being tall enough to do the hood, I was only able to clean the side doors and the tires. The tires, because it was always raining and he drove over puddles, were the dirtiest, grimiest part of the car. In return for leaving them spotless, he let me pretend-drive.

Talo was living with Esperanza, Yiya and Gustavo's ex-daughter-in-law. Actually, my parents said that Esperanza and Yiya and Gustavo's son had never gotten divorced. Esperanza's husband had left for the United States, with their only son, so Esperanza, who didn't want to leave the country and couldn't find another place to live, stayed on with Yiya and Gustavo. They didn't like each other anymore, especially now that she had started living with Talo. Though I had never been inside the house, only to their back yard when Tejedor visited, my parents said Yiya and Esperanza had divided the house in two, with a makeshift wall made of plaster and cardboard.

Sometimes Talo and Esperanza went off on trips and that's when Gustavo would drink *aguardiente,* get drunk, and then play *décimas güajiras* to Yiya. My parents hated those songs because they couldn't stand the way Gustavo slurred the words as he sang. I remember this one time I was up on the fence and Esperanza was hanging the laundry to dry in the patio. She was always telling me to be careful, that I would fall one day and break my head open. (It never happened, not on this wall, anyway; years later, I would break my arm as I walked/balanced on a wrought-iron fence). I turned my attention to her when she drew closer to me on the line. I asked her something or other about Talo's underwear, and she got mad. She called me a *cabroncito*, which I took as diminutive for little goat. Then I told her what I always told her in sing-song, which is why she hated me so much. "Esperanza, Esperanza, esta singa!" It meant something like Esperanza is without gas, but of course it was a play on *cingada,* which meant she was fucked. Then she shot back a mad-as-hell glance and told me she was going to tell my mother what a brat I was.

Talo and Esperanza are still together as far as I know, living in the same house Yiya and Gustavo left behind when they died. I remember them for two reasons: one, because of Talo's car, which ended up taking us to the airport when we left Cuba; and the other, because Esperanza always threatened me with the fact that one day I would pay her back for all the grief and insults I cast at her. Thirty-six years later, remembrance becomes a form of payment.

Cuca

Chain-smoked cigarettes
and after the Revolution
made her own stash from leftover
butts or shredded tobacco leaves,
coughed up phlegm and spat
on the dirt by her feet.
She didn't believe in much,
except the one thing she held true:
that one day she'd leave Cuba.
In the meantime she kept every
single ball that us boys batted
over her fence, enjoyed seeing us
get into hair-pulling, shirt-tearing fights.
She'd smile at us to show us her dentures.
Then one day, as I ran from my father
who was intent on belting me a couple
for being so bad, I ran into her house
and into her bedroom and hid under
her bed. Right there, right there,
as I held my breath and hid from my father
(he had come up to the porch and I could hear
him ask Cuca if she had seen me; she said no,
not knowing I had snuck inside her place)
I bumped into a box. I slid it out from under
the bed, opened its dusty, dog-eared flaps,
and there, there I found all the baseballs
and rubber balls, and tennis balls, scuffed,
browned with age, torn and tattered.
When my father left, I snuck out of Cuca's
house and made a promise not to tell her secret.
A year after she left Cuba, Cuca died of lung
cancer in Miami, Florida, at last free.

Luz & Balmaseda
Street Corner Games

There was *kimbumbia* where we placed one stick
on top of another, like in a cross, then we hit

the stick and watched it soar. Stickball we played
with a broom stick and balled up newspaper

bound tight with string and tape. Dagger
we played with an ice pick which we tossed

high up in the sky and watched for where/how
it landed. Curb ball when we got lucky

and someone got a rubber ball for *Los Reyes*.
Marbles when we found ball bearings or used

smooth, pretty round pebbles. *Caracoles*, or snail
shells: the objective was to knock one against

the other, first shell to cave in lost. When it rained
we made wood boats and raced them in the muddy

currents that ran down the street. Our parents made
papalotes, kites, out of bamboo and rice paper,

with long strips of old bedsheets for tails. We put razor
blades on them or tied broken pieces of bottle and fought

air wars. Those of us with relatives in the United States,
the lucky few of us, received balloons and gum in letters

addressed to our parents. The balloons popped and the gum
made us sick to our stomachs. On the way home one day,

I looked down at the sidewalk and found what I thought
was a balloon, but it turned out to be a used condom.

When my father saw me with the thing in my mouth
as I tried to inflate it, he lost all the color on his cheeks.

He came after me, grabbed the thing out of my mouth,
and threw it away. He couldn't tell me what it was I had

done wrong. How could he begin to explain?
When the games came to an end because by 1969

none of us got toys, or relatives stopped sending
these small gifts, and our imaginations ebbed on dry,

we resorted to flinging rocks at the street lights.
We broke them so many times, the city refused

to replace them. And after that, we built
darts out of chicken feathers, sticks, and needles.

We threw them at each other. Those, too, were taken
away. Everything was taken away, either by parents

or government. The last *Navidades* and *Reyes Magos*
I spent in Cuba, my father got in line for four days

and three nights. When his number came up, one
bicycle was left, which he bought and brought home.

To his son. And what did I do to it? I took the wheels
apart, removed the inner tube, and made the best slingshot

anybody in the neighborhood had seen. Even after the beating
I got from both my mother and father, I became the talk

of the school yard, the talk of the neighborhood. Everyone
agreed I was craziest bastard, with the best slingshot

🐢   *Virgil Suárez*

anybody had ever lain eyes on. No one knocked
out more street lights than I did. No one killed more birds.

No one that entire year wanted to be a better friend to me.
For an only child, what better way to learn the meaning of fickle.

Lazarito & the Habanero Chilis

He was not all there, meaning he had been born
"with problems." That's what our parents said.
His father, all he ever said was, "No, Lázaro. No,
Lázaro. No, Lázaro." But Lázaro was always
getting himself into trouble. He liked to run
out to the streets naked, then he would aim
his peepee out at the cars and urinate in big arcs.
His father would come running out after him,
screaming, "Lázaro, Lázaro, *me vas a volver loco.*"
Then there was the time Lázaro snapped all the
Habanero chilis off the plants that grew in his father's
garden, and he stuffed them in his mouth. Ah, the screams.
His parents had to call the ambulance, and when none
arrived, they asked Talo, our next-door neighbor,
for a ride to the hospital. After the chili incident
we never heard from or saw Lázaro again, and his
parents came and went out of the house
as if they had been childless and content all their lives.

Virgil Suárez

Ricardito

Manuel and Josefina's only son. Like me. We both lived in an imagined world. We played together. He was a couple of years older. A bit slow. As old as he was he drooled and spittle always collected in the corners of his mouth, a frothy gob. We sat by the side of the house and scared each other with ghost stories. While we told stories, we played with the mud-turned-clay in his mother's garden, which wasn't a garden at all but a strip of earth between the house wall and the fence. There coffee plants grew, and it was here where we made clay soldiers and we fought wars, and because he was older he always won. One day, and this my mother still claims, I got so mad at him that I filled my milk bottle with urine, then I told Ricardito that it was orange juice and, being thirsty, he drank it. I don't remember this story, but my mother says it is true. Josefina and Manuel, she says, had a good laugh. They were always doing that, it seemed, laughing at their one and only son. My mother, whenever she needed to give me a shot, took me over to Ricardito's where she proceeded to bend me over her knees and then inject whatever it was that I needed. Those, too, were the days that both Ricardito and I were always taking something that was supposed to be "so good" for our health. Our mother's gave us Scott's Cod Liver Emulsion, all kinds of vitamin's, *jarabes* for growth and stamina. Funny how none of it helped in terms of the distance and the different lives Ricardito and I have lived. Him, still in Cuba; me, in the United States. Him finding his own mother dead in her bedroom three days after she had died of a heart attack. All the time the tetracycline our mothers took during pregnancy turning our teeth yellow-green. I also have a lasting image of him on the day I learned how to ride my bicycle without its training wheels. As I took off, he ran after me, in the clumsy way children with orthopaedic boots do, shouting, *"Dale, Dale, Dale!"* Still today, as my own daughter learns to pedal her bike, I cannot help but run after her, shouting, *"Dale, Dale,"* and I think of Ricardito still in Cuba.

Virgil Suárez

Jicotea/Turtle

They arrived in yute sacks. Their carapaces forming lumps as they pushed against the weaved string of the brown sacks. Once my father had put down the sack on the cemented patio of the house in Havana, I walked around the lumpy pile, intrigued. I was still at the age of endless questions. My father said he'd gotten lucky this time at La Ciénega de Zapata, a pocket of the province of Las Villas. My father was from this swampy area of the island of Cuba. "What is it?" I asked. *"Jicoteas,"* he said, and smiled, then reached into his shirt pocket for a cigarette. This was the time when my father still smoked, despite his bouts with asthma. Jico . . . I began but my tongue stumbled over the word . . . *teas? "Tortuguitas,"* he said. "Let me show you one." He opened the mouth of the sack and reached into it the way a magician might into his hat to pull out a fluttering white dove. It appeared: a turtle. Startled, waving its claws? feet? legs? in the air as if making a futile attempt at swimming or escaping. "See?" my father asked. "Surely you've been shown pictures at school." (At school we'd only been shown pictures of Camilo

Cienfuegos, Che Guevara, Jose Martí, Karl Marx, Máximo Gómez, Vladimir Lenin, etc . . .) "Give me a hand," he said. At first I was reluctant, but then my father turned the sack upside down and let about thirty of these turtles free. "But they'll get away," I told him. And again, he smiled, then blew smoke out of his nostrils. "No, no, no," he said. "See how they move? They are slow. They can't get away fast enough." Get away from what, I thought. Indeed, these slowpoke creatures tried to make a path on the cemented patio and, I swear, made little scratch sounds with their nails against the surface. My father crushed the cigarette under his shoe, reached to the sheath tied to the side of his right thigh and pulled out his sharp machete. "This is what I want you to do, son," he said, and showed me. He grabbed one of the turtles, stepped on it so that it could not move, then with his free hand he pulled and extended the neck of the turtle. "Like this, see?" He stretched. I looked, not catching on yet. Then, to my surprise, he swung the machete downward fast. There was a loud crushing sound. There was a spark as the machete sliced through the turtle's neck and hit the hard concrete underneath. The stub of the creature's neck lay on the floor like a piece of rotted plantain. It was still twitching as I looked up at my father, who was saying, "It's that simple; you grab and pull and I chop." As reluctant as I was, I did as I was told. I grabbed every one of those thirty turtles' necks, pulled without looking into their eyes, and closed mine each of the thirty times the machete came down. Turtle, after turtle, after turtle. All thirty. "After this you help me clean up, no?" my father was saying. "We need to remove the shells so that your mother can clean the meat and cook it." Yes, we were going to eat these turtles, these *jicoteas* (the sound of the word now comes naturally). There was nothing I could say on behalf of the creatures I had helped my father slaughter. And so the idea of death had been inflicted upon me quickly, almost painlessly, with the sacrifice of thirty *jicoteas*.

🐢   Virgil Suárez

Bitterness

My father brings home the blood of horses on his hands, his rough, calloused, thick-fingered hands. He comes home from the slaughterhouse where the government pays him to kill old useless horses that arrive from all over the island. The blood comes encrusted and etched on the prints and wrinkles of his fingers, under his nails, dark with the dirt, too, the filth and grime, the moons of his fingers pinked by the residue, his knuckles skinned from the endless work. Sticky and sweet-scented is the blood of these horses, horses to feed the lions in the new zoo which is moving from Havana to Lenin's Park, near where we live. Dark blood, this blood of the horses my father slaughters daily to feed zoo lions. I ask how many horses it takes to feed a single lion. This makes my father laugh. I watch as he washes and rinses the dried-up blood from his forearms and hands, those hands that kill the horses, the hands that sever through skin and flesh and crush through bone. My father, the dissident, the *gusano*, the Yankee-lover, walks to and from work on tired feet, on an aching body. He no longer talks to anybody, and less to us, his family. My mother and my grandmother, his mother. But they leave him alone, to his moods, for they know what he is being put through. A test of will. Determination. Salvation and survival. My father, under the tent on the grounds of the new zoo, doesn't say much. He has learned how to speak with his hands. Sharp are the cuts he makes on the flesh. The horses are shot in the open fields, a bullet through the head, and are then carted to where my father, along with other men, do the butchering. He is thirty (the age I am now) and tired, and when he comes home his hands are numb from all the chopping and cutting. This takes place in 1969.

🐢 🐢 🐢

Years later when we are allowed to leave Cuba and travel to Madrid, to the cold winter of Spain, we find ourselves living in a hospice. The three of us, my father, mother and me, in a small room. (My grandmother died and was buried in Havana.) Next door is a man named Izquierdo, who keeps us awake with his phlegmy coughs. From the other side of the walls, his coughing sounds like thunder. We try to sleep; I try harder but the coughing seeps through and my father curses under his breath. I listen to the heat as it tic-tacs coming through the furnace. My father tries to make love to my mother. I try not to listen. The mattress springs sound like bones crushing. My mother refuses without saying a word. This is the final time she does so tonight. There is what seems like an interminable silence, then my father breaks it by saying to my mother, "If you don't, I'll look for a Spanish woman who will." Silence again, then I think I hear my mother crying. "Someone," my father says, "will want to, to . . ." And I lay there on my edge of the mattress, sweat coming on from the heat. My eyes are closed and I listen hard, and then the sound of everything stops. This, I think, is the way death must sound. Then

Virgil Suárez

my father begins all over again. The room fills with the small sounds . . . the cleaver falls and cuts through the skin, tears through the flesh, crushes the bone, and then there is the blood. All that blood. It emerges and collects on the slaughter tables, the blood of countless horses.

Sleep upon me, I see my father stand by the sink in the patio of the house in Havana. He scrubs and rinses his hands. The blood dissolves slowly in the water. Once again I build up the courage to go ahead and ask him how much horse meat it takes to appease the hunger of a single lion.

Uncle Isidoro

not really an uncle
but my mother's second cousin
me & my cousins called him *Tío*
he sat on the rocking chair all day
taught the parrot to talk
say bad words after people's names
smoked handrolled cigarettes
blew huge smoke rings
that floated unbroken to the ceiling
he sat & rocked & drank espresso
every time my aunt Silvia brewed it
after the revolution he got recruited
to cut sugarcane in the fields
the work took a thin man & made
him thinner killed him
after his death my aunt
didn't let anyone sit in *his* chair
and when she brewed coffee
she always poured a little
in his cup & left it by the chair
my aunt Silvia claimed
Isidoro moved through the house
as a *sapo* we never believed
her until the night we heard
a bullfrog croak & then the parrot
stirred awake & called out
Isidoro's name

Virgil Suárez

Bay of Pigs Revisited

*In 1966 Aunt Aleida came to visit Havana because she
was getting married in Las Villas and she wanted my
mother, the seamstress, to make her a dress from a
special piece of cloth for which one of my mother's sisters had traded two pigs and a goat. The piece of cloth
was a parachute that had fallen out of the sky during
the Bay of Pigs invasion. All that remained of the sur-
vivor was a fading hand print. My mother and aunt
told stories as to what had been the fate of the para-
chuter as he plummeted from the sky onto a hostile
beach. Surely, they contemplated, he died in the strug
gle and this was his hand, pinked onto the material by
the soldier's blood.*

none of us knew the color of the ground
when we fell from the sky, hung
in the air, parachutes opening like Medusas,
while the sound of the planes faded

bullets pierced the skin, riddled our bodies
as we fell onto the sand, we fell dead, wounded,
in *camara lenta*, onto the sand, our blood
stained and dissolved in familiar waters

we stood and delivered until every magazine
emptied, cease fire called, we dropped our weapons
and surrendered, walked under palms
up the beach, hands up behind our heads,

Spared Angola

boots sinking in the sand, while black birds flew
over the strewn corpses, and some, stuffed,
perched on the broken bodies, preened their feathers
others pecked tongues and plucked eyes

of familiar faces, we, the survivors, moved
single file down the beach as we listened
to the silence that arose from the shore
to the silence that arose from the shores of exile

Virgil Suárez

Pin Pan Pun

Is Cuban Spanish for spring-sprung bed. *A catre* upon which so many of the relatives rested their weary bodies when they visited our house in Havana from the Provinces in Cuba. They would come to the city to spend a few weeks with us. Uncles, aunts, cousins, second cousins. They all came and slept on those squeaky, spring-bound little beds my parents kept for such visits. We owned four or five in total. And they seemed to be used all the time. My cousins loved to roll me up and sandwich me in the folds of the gray mattresses. Trapped there, they tickled me and sometimes made me pee in my pajamas. We laughed so hard as children, sometimes the laughing brought on coughing and asthma attacks, not mine but my cousins. The *"pin-pan-puns,"* as my parents called them, were priceless, like our television set and our radio, because they stopped coming into the country after the revolution in 1959. "After," my father said so all the time, "everything has stopped coming into the country." My mother and aunts agreed. Nothing new coming in. Everything scarce. Nowhere to be bought or traded. Things grew worse every day.

But we had our little, spring-noisy beds, and so people continued to visit us. It was great fun as all the summers ran together. People sleeping in all the different rooms of the house. Lots of coughing, sneezing and whispering. These noises of intense human moments. The springs uttered their complaints under the weight of bodies. My cousins laughed, and when the noises stopped—we all slept together on the floor in my room—we tickled each other and spoke in hushed voices of scary things we saw in the dark. In the middle of the night we would sneak out of my room and tiptoe around the house, sneaking and listening for adult sounds. The little beds under the billowing, cone-shaped mosquito nets looked like great big animals. Monsters. It was breathless fun to run around the house in the dark, in the silence of so many adults asleep, snoring, tossing and turning in their sleep. We pretended to be mice, the little ones, and we hid from the big cat, our oldest cousin, Jaime. In the morning while we slept, the adults got up, drank the coffee my mother made, talked, and they would gather up and put away all the little beds, so that when we woke up it would all seem like a dream. Even now, from the distance of my own adulthood, they *have* become a dream, these memories of the *pin-pan-puns*.

Virgil Suárez

Leo

owner of the kiosk in Arroyo Naranjo.
She tended her shop & made her living
& introduced me to sweets: *melcocha,*
boniatillo, dulce de coco, guarapo.
When my father gathered with his friends
at the corner kiosk, they often spoke
among themselves about things
better left unspoken: anti-revolution
talk, the kind that got you killed
if someone heard & snitched.
So Leo, outspoken & brave,
braver than all those men who drank
her *cafecitos,* never opted for silence.
She spoke her mind on things
& spoke out loud. Wasn't afraid.
& the men liked her because like them
she was *gusano* & like them she liked women
& like most of them her fate became
imprisonment & later, not too much later,
death. The kiosk was boarded up
& left to rot & so for the children
of Arroyo Naranjo, there would never
be any more sweets & for the men
no place to gather & talk & plot
some essentials that kept so many
going back to Leo's kiosk.

Yiya & Gustavo

our Havana next-door neighbors
whenever she walked to the market
us kids sang: *"Yiya, Yiya*
Mantequilla, está loca . . ."
& she'd curse at us
Gustavo drank *aguardiente*
real rotgut & on his guitar
played *décimas guajiras*
from the back yard
next door: *"Yiya, Yiya*
Mantequilla."
& there'd be a silence so great
sometime after the revolution
& Gustavo's arrest & imprisonment
Yiya never left the house
& in the wake of her retreat
left nothing but Gustavo's
clothes on the wash line
rain or shine & the wind
played & made the shirts billow
& while we played in our yard,
we'd hear the faint sounds
"Yiya, Yiya, Mantequilla."

Virgil Suárez

Gutiérrez

My father's friend who owned the rusty, noisy Indian motorcycle and came to visit the house a couple of times a week. He'd arrive and help my father with the animals. Often, he'd let me sit on the motorcycle and pretend I was riding it. Even though my father never said so, Gutiérrez was the closest friend my father came to having in those uncertain days after the revolution. Gutiérrez, a short, stocky, dark-skin man with a crown of graying hair around a big bald spot. Gutiérrez of the big cigars and the scent of his smoke which followed him everywhere he went. Sometimes, if the wind blew in the right direction, the smell preceded his arrival. He arrived and parked his motorcycle in front of the house. "Take good care of it, *muchacho*," he said to me as he passed by on the porch and entered the house. Soon enough, some of the other kids from the neighborhood appeared and I bragged to them about how one day the bike, Gutiérrez's bike, would be mine. It seemed then like the only way to regain their respect, or make them jealous for having treated me like an outcast at school. According to the government, my parents and I were anti-social element because we wanted to leave the country or rather, my parents had decided to take me out of the country before I ended up fighting in Angola, Cuba's own Viet Nam. My father smoked cigarettes in those days, so he and Gutiérrez, after doing whatever it was they did in the patio, sat and smoked and talked about politics and the revolution in a roundabout way. Sometimes they communicated without really speaking, with hums, tsk-tsks and guttural laugher. Or nodded some truth or another into being. Both he and my father were counter-revolutionaries, or *gusanos,* which was what the government called people like us, dissidents opposed to the revolution. They sat on the porch steps next to the banana trees and planned ways of leaving and taking their families out. But Gutiérrez couldn't really leave because he was married to Teresa, "the witch," as he called her. They had children together, and because of that he couldn't leave. Teresa, he told my father often, was a stubborn woman—he hated her with a passion, or so he said. Sometimes he'd catch up to me at the beginning of our block and give me a ride home. I'd hold on tight, my face and chest against his damp back. Straddling the seat, I'd feel the grunts and rumbles of the engine vibrate through me as we rode over potholes and rocks. Ah, the excitement of the first push and then there was movement as we rolled over the pebbled dirt road past all the houses. I knew well that the other children heard the sound of the motorcycle and ran to their windows to look out, to watch me pass by, riding on Gutiérrez's bike. Gutiérrez picked up speed right before we got to the house. Then he would wave to my father and ride off. Of course, long after I went inside, I could still smell the smoke of Gutiérrez's cigar everywhere. Those were the days when I wanted nothing more than to be a spy and ride a motorcycle.

🐢 🐢 🐢

Virgil Suárez

I remember that when I joined my father and Gutiérrez on the porch, the cigar smoke was so potent that it made me dizzy. Both he and my father claimed it kept the mosquitoes away. Other bugs, too. "How about frogs?" I'd ask, having developed one of my many childhood-adulthood fears. "Frogs ,too," Gutiérrez would say, and then wink at me. He and my father sat there, wrapped in the smoke and aroma. They talked of the possibilities and what-ifs. Then, after what seemed like a long time, Gutiérrez would point to me and say to my father, "He needs a better future." My father nodded in agreement. "It'll be a shame if this kid ends up in the military. Who knows what'll happen to him then?" My father grew serious because he often entertained the possibility of my getting involved in the *Pioneritos* (a cross between the Boy Scouts of America and the Hitler Youth) at the age of fifteen, then getting drafted into the Army. Once he thought about it too much, it didn't matter if he was finishing a cigarette or starting a new one, he placed the thing under his foot and ground it out. *"Hijos de puta,"* my father would say under his breath, smoke leaving his nostrils. "No way they'll get their hands on my boy." To change the conversation as he stood up to leave, Gutiérrez would ask me if I wanted a ride on his bike. Thus the long awaited moment through the riddles of conversation and hypnotic smoke. Yes! He climbed on first, kicked the pedal and started the engine, then he pulled me up and over behind him. I held on to the belt loops on his pants, and off we rode up and down the barrio street several times until he dropped me off again and waved goodbye. How many times did I not stand there and watch him fade into the distance.

🐢 🐢 🐢

Gutiérrez stopped coming by the house one day, and I overheard my father tell my mother the reason why. Gutiérrez and his wife were getting divorced, and he was going through hard times. "She's accused him," my father told my mother, "of counter-revolutionary activities. The police came and arrested him." After that, my parents never mentioned Gutiérrez again, at least not in my presence, and Gutiérrez never rode by again and never came to visit.

🐢 🐢 🐢

My father went through a moody period when all he did was sit on the porch and smoke his cigarettes and curse at nothing under his breath. He and I knew it was no use; without Gutiérrez there was something missing. Hopes in conversation for my father, for me the chance to show off on his motorcycle.

🐢 🐢 🐢

Many years later when my parents lived in Hialeah, Florida, and I was visiting them from college, there was a knock at the door. I answered it as I was on my way out. It was a man who claimed he knew my father. I called my father, and he came to the door. As I was about to leave, I saw my father and this man embrace. The man started to cry. My father invited him in. "Do you know who this is?" he asked me. I couldn't place the face. "This is Gutiérrez's son," he said. I shook the man's hand and out of respect I followed them inside and sat with him and my father. I sat there looking for resemblances, but there were none. The son in front of me looked nothing like the father I knew in my childhood. He told my father that Gutiérrez had gone insane and that he had died in the asylum. "It was a terrible thing," the son said. The three of us sat in silence, and then my father asked me, "Do you remember Gutiérrez?" There was more silence because remembering was easy. Then the son asked me, "Do you? Do you remember my father?" "I remember his motorcycle . . ." I began. His son smiled, then grew serious and said, "They took it away from him. They confiscated it. They stole it like they stole everything from everybody." But not the memories, I thought, those we keep, like Gutiérrez on his bike, heading up hill, into the horizon, riding on into the distance, against all forgetting. *In pace requiescat. En paz descanse.*

The End of the World according to Babio

imagine
gasoline rains
from the sky
imagine
two fireflies
collide
in the night
their spark
& the fumes
from the gas
set this whole
earth on fire
imagine that

Virgil Suárez

La Santa

takes her morning walk
& returns by noon
to feed her cat
she slowly opens
the canned liver
& scoops it
silver clean
the cat sits
& stares & licks
its whiskers
as she takes 2 paper
plates & equally
divides the food
among them
she chews a spoonful
& swallows
the cat merely
sits & stares

The Goat Incident

One of the biggest scars from my childhood comes at my most vulnerable moment. I'm still clueless about the reasons, though I have speculated: the government's torment of my father (he was going crazy, I remember, once having tried to set the house on fire, though that's another story), the friction between my mother and father due to my grandmother's illness, the fact that my parents had been trying to leave the island for the last few years, since 1962 (the year I was born). They had left me in the care of my maternal grandparents in the little town of San Pablo, somewhere in the Province of Las Villas. I cannot remember how I got there, whether my parents brought me or somebody went to Havana and picked me up. Funny how memory fails one.

🐢 🐢 🐢

But the goat incident I remember well from all the years that I've had to carry it blazoned in my memory, though I once tried to purge myself of it in one of my books, my first novel, in fact, a pseudo autobiography, not mine but my father's. I claim this because I was too young to go through any of what the main character, Julián Campos in *The Cutter,* went through. But my father did. It was his life mostly that I tried to capture in that book. Anyway, I wrote a chapter about the goat incident, which I liked and my agent liked—she thought it added dimension—but when it came to my editor, he thought it didn't fit. So, I cut it out, for a few drafts, but then reworked it into another form. Having it printed in another form didn't resolve the scarring, so I've carried it with me since. I've carried it since 1968, when I was six and somehow I had ended up in the care of my maternal grandparents.

🐢 🐢 🐢

The incident begins very much like the chapter I wrote in the novel with an unknown voice. An unknown, unseen voice saying, "Let's go, let's go, there's a fight. Let's go see it." My grandfather, Domingo, white-haired then (as he is now more than twenty years later), climbed onto his horse. My mother's brothers were there and they too got on their horses. I looked up at these giants sitting on these beasts. I wanted to go, too. I voiced so to my grandfather. He turned the horse a few times, then he reached down and in one swoop he pulled me up and I found myself sitting behind him, holding on to him. They wasted no time going up to wherever it was the fight had broken out. I embraced my grandfather. I felt the horse hair sneaking in through my pants and irritating the skin on my legs. In the novel, the incident took place at night, but such violence was better seen by a child at night and then attributed to nightmares, but in broad daylight . . . what torment.

☗ ☗ ☗

We arrived in a clearing which was surrounded by *bohíos,* which were thatched huts. A crowd of men made a circle. When we rode up, I was able to catch some of the action before my grandfather dismounted his horse and then pulled me off and asked me to stay away at a distance. There were two men, that much I saw. They stood in the circle, bare chested, shoeless. The circle of men expanded and contracted as the pushing and shoving continued. Again, the men in the circle. Another glimpse revealed the men, sweating, bestial, fighting each other with goats. With goats over their shoulders. Both goats had not made it. They were limp in death. One of the animals was white. The other spotted, or was that blood? I pulled my grandfather's horse away. Both my uncles were pushing their way into the circle. I ran to a nearby guava tree, tied my grandfather's horse to it, and climbed up high on to one of the branches. A part of me didn't want to see, but the other did, and so I climbed higher, scraping the insides of my thighs against the knobby branches of the tree. I went up high enough to get a perfect view.

☗ ☗ ☗

Inside the circle of spectators, the two men went about their fighting slowly. The fight had been going on for quite some time now, for the men moved sluggishly as if tired and worn-out. One goat's belly had been gutted open by the horns of the other. The pink and reddish entrails dangled like rope out of the gaping wound. They oozed over the bare-backed man. The other goat had its fur stained. Their heads hung limp.

☗ ☗ ☗

Virgil Suárez

"I'll kill you," the man with the gutted goat said. "I'll teach you to respect a man." The other man did not respond. He charged and struck the other man with the goat. The other man lost his balance. He fell on his knees, but then got up quickly and charged. No one made an attempt to stop the two men from fighting. I hung tightly, wondering when my grandfather and uncles would come to the rescue. For the goats, they had arrived too late, but not for the men.

Someone threw in a knife. The one man with the spotted goat flung the carcass off his shoulders and picked up the knife. The men continued now with their death dance. The man with the knife kept stabbing at the goat. More blood, more entrails. Then a machete was thrown in to the other man. He let go of the mangled goat and grabbed the machete. Both men swung at each other. The one with the knife swung low at the other's stomach, each time missing, coming close the next. This went on and on until one of the men lost his balance, perhaps out of exhaustion, and fell on his back. The other man, the one with the machete, swung and cut the man on the arm. The sharp blade cut through the flesh down to the bone.

🐢 🐢 🐢

The crowd held its breath. For one long moment all sound escaped the scene. Then my grandfather fired a shot and the crowd parted. My uncles took their place by both men. Why my grandfather waited so long to fire, I still don't know. He and my uncles stood in the center of the circle and kept both men from starting again. My grandfather told everyone to go away, to go back to their homes. The men did reluctantly at first, but then, seeing how my grandfather and uncles were serious, more quickly.

🐢 🐢 🐢

Then I can't remember much else, other than looking down and realizing how high up in the tree I had climbed. How would I get down? I started to inch my way down slowly. My hands became tired and cramped. Slowly I came down, my inner thighs on fire, scraped and bruised. I made it down and grabbed the horse's bit and pulled him away from the tree. My grandfather and uncles returned. We all got on the horses and rode back to my grandparents' house. I rode back holding on to my grandfather's waist, my head against his chest. I listened to him as he talked to my uncles about what had happened. Why the men had fought. The one man had caught the other with his wife. My uncles laughed and nodded their heads. "These *guajiros*," my grandfather said, "they have too much time on their hands." My uncles nodded in agreement.

🐢 🐢 🐢

We arrived at the house, and the men told nothing to the women. The women, my aunts and grandmother, had heard the shots, so they wanted to know what happened. "Let's eat," my grandfather said. I wanted to hear it again, the whole story. Over dinner, my grandfather spoke up and told of what had happened, but I couldn't make it out, the conversation being too adult for my understanding. I kept waiting and waiting for him to mention the goats, but he didn't mention them. I kept hearing about violence, the violence of these men so secluded from society. This was the kind of violence, my grandfather must have said, that was brought about by the system. And much later that night I thought about the goats. As on so many other countless nights to follow, I thought about the dead goats. The way their heads dangled, eyes wide open, tongues sticking out from the corners of their mouths. Years later, when I saw Francis Ford Coppola's *Apocalypse Now,* in the scene where the natives kill the oxen during a

Virgil Suárez

ceremony, I thought of the goat incident again. I then realized what I believe about violence now: it is all irrational, it is not supposed to make sense after the fact. After so many years, even words, language fails to relate what really did happen, what memory and recollection choose to carve out into some deep recess of ourselves.

Xagua Castle, Cienfuegos

S its on top of a high cliff overlooking the bay in which the docked boats stretch and dry their nets. The child stares at it from the balcony of some relative's house. His grandmother is there with him. She rocks on a wicker rocking chair behind him and tells him about the treasures Cook's pirates hid in the castle long ago. "Will you take me to see them?" the child asks. "Maybe tomorrow. It's too late and the ghosts are taking care of it now." The child asks if his grandmother was alive when they built the castle. She tells him no and takes his hand. "I wasn't born yet. The Spaniards built it." The child asks who the Spaniards were, were they good? Sometimes, she tells him, sometimes they didn't understand other people. The other people were the Indians. The Indians *were* the noblest of people. They didn't bother anyone, lived free to hunt and raise their families. "I want to see the ghosts," the child says. The grandmother assures him that if he looks hard enough he can see them from there. She smooths the wrinkles on her dress, gets up and goes inside. The child sits with his legs dangling between the wrought-iron bars of the veranda while he admires the castle. The darker it grows, the more he believes he can see ghosts floating in and out of the high towers.

Izquierdo

The phlegmy coughs resounded and echoed in the lazy afternoon hours when I was home from school. Izquierdo wore nothing but shorts and a stained undershirt. No matter the weather, he always sat on the sofa of the hostel rooms he and his wife Eloísa and my parents and I shared. Izquierdo was dying of throat cancer, but he wouldn't stop smoking cigarettes and, whenever he wanted to make his wife suffer, cigars, the cheap stinky kind that left an awful stench on all my clothes. He sat on the sofa in silence, smoking and nodding at the plumes of smoke that whirled into his eyes. He continued to smoke, even when the doctor had told him not to do it anymore, even when he knew it was too late to stop because he was dying. But he didn't *want* to stop. "Period," as he would put it. "*¡Punto y aparte!*" And Eloísa would leave each time he sat there smoking, for she couldn't stand the sight of him killing himself.

My parents didn't know it, but many an afternoon I would spy on Izquierdo smoking and nodding and sometimes muttering to himself in his native Cuban Spanish, once in a while a *"coño"* becoming audible. All he ever talked about was what he had lost . . . his homeland . . . his house . . . his/his/his. I would spy on him to make sure that he would not be using the bathroom anytime soon, since I was twelve and afternoons had become my time to masturbate. This was my secret. The way Izquierdo smoked, I masturbated.

Through the bathroom door I would hear him cough, loud grinding and wheezing coughs. Izquierdo sat there throughout the winter, spring and well into summer, smoking, smoking, smoking—leaving a trail of ashes and tobacco all over the living room and hallway that ended at the entrance of his and Eloísa's room. Eloísa once told him that if he saved all the cigarette butts of cigarettes he had consumed, he could fill many buckets. "You've filled your lungs," she said to him one afternoon, "with that poison, and I want no part of it. *¿Me oyes?*"

🐢 🐢 🐢

That was the same afternoon that I went into the bathroom for the last time (I didn't know it would be the last time I would masturbate in the bathroom, that bathroom anyway). I closed the door and there came a great silence while I put my hands to work. Left first, then right, then both. Those were days of ambidexterity. Suddenly I heard footsteps approach on the other side of the door, then they stopped. Izquierdo, I thought. He tapped on the door and said, "We're going to have to put bells around your wrists." Then he walked away. I didn't know what he meant, but I did stop and stood up and raised and buckled my pants and walked out of the bathroom a little embarrassed, as if he had been able to see what I was doing through the door. The next time he saw me, which was a couple of days later, he smiled behind a few puffs of smoke, looked at me from across the smoke-filled room and said, "Good afternoon, Jingle Bells." I returned to the room I shared with my parents and sat on the bed confused, for I was beginning to understand what he had meant. *Jingle bells.*

Virgil Suárez

In Praise of Mentors
or How I Became a Cuban-American Writer

For Jerome H. Stern,
Writer, mentor, teacher, friend
September 27, 1938 - March 19, 1996

I.

In 1970, when I turned eight, my paternal grandmother Isabel fell ill. I didn't know what ailed her or why she was sick, but my parents decided that it would be best to keep the door to her room closed, and did their best always to keep me—during those brief moments when they did open her door—from taking a peek inside. Whenever I asked what was wrong, the answer was "your grandmother doesn't feel well, *está viejita.*"

I have, having come upon some difficult moments in my own life, forgiven my parents for their lack of understanding and knowledge of child psychology. They didn't know that to keep what ailed my grandmother from me behind a closed door would have a profound psychological effect upon me. I understand now. They were trying very hard to spare their only child from being exposed to one of life's cruelest realities: people get old and die, and sometimes the ways by which the old die are painful to watch.

At the time in Havana, Cuba, my parents went through some of the most tense moments of their lives. My father, a policeman during Batista's regime, was being persecuted because he wanted no part of the Cuban Revolution and its leader, Fidel Castro. By extension, we were all looked upon as *"gusanos,"* which literally means worm, and which was the name given by the government to people like us who wanted to leave the island. My mother, who didn't work outside the house, spent her days inventing and concocting the family's next meal. She was forever foraging, *fujilateando,* the market places for chicken, bits of *bacalao*, or *tasajo* with which to make my grandmother soup or *ajiaco*, something potent to uplift everybody's spirits during these rough days. She also took care of my grandmother's needs, which involved, I imagined in those days of childhood innocence, going into the room to read her stories from *Granma* or *Bohemia*, the only newspaper and magazine, to keep my grandmother informed of what was going on outside her bedroom walls.

I have come to believe that the years between 1965 and 1970 were important years in my development as a writer. Those years of solitude and introvertedness—for a child who was an involuntary outcast and who learned quickly that the best way to pass the time was to utilize his imagination—left their indelible mark upon me, a sort of Grand Canyon of emotional scars. Being alone gave me the proper tools to heed the voices, prop up the ghosts, create the characters who later would haunt me, and probably will for the rest of my days.

My grandmother helped me exercise my imagination. Before she grew ill, she taught me the tools necessary. Thus I considered her my first mentor. Not only did she help me to get started by telling me stories, but she also taught me the ways to listen to sounds. Tropical places have their own beats and rhythms like rain falling upon the fronds of a banana plant, falling on corrugated tin roofs, on troughs, which was, like she said, the sound of galloping horses. Like hands clapping. Like, if I cupped my hands over my ears, the waves crashing against the shoreline. The dried leaves of coffee plants, she said, spoke as the wind dragged them across our cemented patio.

She was the first person who taught me to see.

Often, she pointed to the clouds on rainy days and she asked me what I though a particular cloud formation looked like. Most afternoons were spent spotting animals and things in the cotton-like clouds. She named things for the first time. The *lagartija* (lizard), the *cucuyo* (firefly), the *gorreón* (sparrow). She told me that a lot of our words sounded like African chants. The influence of Africa upon the island of Cuba is unmistakably what has most enriched us, a people adrift having been cut off from our aboriginal past. *"Un bache,"* she said, which literally translates into a pothole in the road. If spoken fast, becomes *unbache-unbacheunbache*, and does have a chant-like, mesmerizing quality to its sound.

By naming the colors, she gave birth to them: the green of *papayas,* the yellow of *mango* meat, the red orange of the *mamey.* In her hands, my imaginative powers flourished, for my grandmother was not only a good storyteller, but a magician as well. She showed me card and coin tricks, long forgotten now because I no longer have the ability to suspend my disbelief. I am too jaded and pessimistic, but back then I possessed the agility and quickness of mind necessary to believe in slight-of-hand tricks.

Spared Angola

Ah, the things she could carve with her fingernails on a piece of modeling clay. She'd pinch here and there and right before my eyes would appear an elephant, a horse, a duck, or a rabbit. And what couldn't she do with a piece of paper. It wasn't until years later that I realized my grandmother knew *origami*, the Japanese art of paper sculpting. She drew with charcoal and painted with watercolors; she sang: *"Ay Mamá Inés, Ay Mamá Inés, todos los negros tomamos cafe";* she knew fun games.

In her were the nine muses, rebelling against boredom.

My grandmother possessed the secret of balance. She built these huge houses of cards with the steadiest of hands. In her fingers a pencil or a spoon wobbled with surprising fluidity. A teacher most of her adult life, she knew how to maintain a child's attention. She knew how to feed and nourish my imagination. If memories are what preserve the images of those gone from this world, then I believe my grandmother is still with me, as a guide, a guardian angel (though I'm no longer religious), a mentor. Back then, most of the time, I was hypnotized by her voice (*"tin marín de dos pingües, cúcara mácara títere fue!"*), by the fragrances of the linden-flower tea she drank on her breath, by the loose skin on the back of her arms that hung down like turkey gobblers. Though wrinkled by time and hard work, her hands and fingers, for me, felt as soft as a sparrow's down feather.

Though time seems endless in childhood, all good things come to an end. My grandmother fell ill and retreated deeper into the darkness of her room, surrendered to the darkness in her mind. The last few weeks of her life, as I remember, she screamed from behind the door, cursed at those whom she no longer recognized or mistook for other people, summoned people already dead. My mother kept rushing in and out of that room. My father, too, came and went, sometimes crying, out of his mother's room. She was dying and no one was brave enough to tell me the truth.

🌼   *Virgil Suárez*

My grandmother, Aurelia Isabel García González, died on July 20, 1970, a few months before we were all granted exit visas and could leave Havana for Madrid, Spain. All I remember is not seeing her after they took her away in the ambulance. She never came back from the hospital, and my parents took a long time to say she would not be coming back from where she had gone. At night, I prayed and listened, and from outside, as the rain fell at night, I swear I could hear her voice, a susurrus beckoning me to dream and imagine.

II.

Much later, having been exposed to what happens to people, old people especially, in hospitals, I put two and two together and understood the "little accidents," as my mother called illness and dying, to be absolute horrors and humiliations aging brings and of which my parents tried their hardest to spare me, like they later tried to spare me of going to war in Angola (Cuba's Vietnam) by taking me out of the country. I guess all the years of trying to find out what was going on behind a closed door exercised and developed my imagination. But, imagination alone does not make one a better writer. One needs mentors to keep one guided, inspired, focused, enthusiastic about the work at hand—that long winding road which leads to the endless perils or pleasures.

From the very beginning of my development as a writer, I have been lucky, fortunate indeed to have had such good mentors in my life. My grandmother was one. I think through their hard work and hope, my parents were others. There was also Andres Pardillo, my paternal cousin's husband who for *Los Reyes Magos*, months before my grandmother died, brought me a box full of books, illustrated, abridged, and translated American and French literature classics. At the age of eight I read *Moby Dick, The Legend of Sleepy Hollow, The Count of Monte Cristo, The Hunchbach of Notre Dame,* and *Cyrano de Bergerac*. There was most of Jules Verne, too, whose books I read and reread for weeks.

When we traveled to Spain, I received as formal an education as my parents could afford, focused mostly in math and science, my two life-long weaknesses. Most of the language basics I learned I couldn't keep straight. Even to this day, I cannot understand the concept of accents or when to use *v* instead of *b*, as in *vaca*, and *y* or *ll*, as in *lluvia*. Perhaps these problems were the reason why switching over to English, as a language within which to think and write, was so easy. I learned early not to get hung up with so much language stuff. Language works, for me, on the level of music. I didn't learn much during those four splendid years in Spain, but God did I gather memories. Like my parents, I lived, lived with gusto and delight of this new life, though I was too young to understand that Spain was still ruled by fascist Franco.

Later, having moved to the United States and settled in Los Angeles, California, as a high school student at Huntington Park Senior High School, I found myself in Advance Placement Spanish with Mr. Enrique Alvarado as a teacher.

Mr. Alvarado taught me that writing can be fun. I wrote poetry in Spanish in those days. Poems I am glad I have lost or thrown away. *Señor* Alvarado taught his students to write from models. And what models he exposed us to! In class we read not only the classics like *El Cid* and Jorge Manrique's *Rimas* for his dead father, but the 20th Century writers, most importantly those writers emanating from Latin America: Gabriel García Márquez, Carlos Fuentes, Jorge Luis Borges, Alejo Carpentier, Gabriela Minstral, Pablo Neruda, and the Spanish Federico Garcia Lorca.

We read *Poet In New York*. I knew then I wanted to write poetry. I fell in love with the power to charm words possess. Lorca was Alvarado's favorite. When he spoke about the great poet, his eyes watered, his voice grew soft and it cracked with the regret of humanity having lost such a great poet, so young. We read not only the poetry by Lorca, but his plays as well:

Blood Wedding, The House of Bernarda Alba (which reminded me of my maternal grandmother who is still living in Cuba), and *Yerma.*

Alvarado took us by the hand and showed us the sounds of the words in Spanish. I learned that most important step after acquiring the powers of imagination, one needs to read. Read everything all the time. "Read," Alvarado often told us before the bell rang, "like you eat when you are hungry. Read VORACIOUSLY! And if that doesn't work, as always there will be a *quiz.*" He pronounced quiz by stretching it out like a photographer's *cheeeeese.*

In the same high school, there was also Joel Goldstock, my tenth-grade English teacher, who entertained us with his eccentric wacky ways—he often stirred his coffee with a pen or pencil, once, even, with the handle of a pointer. Mr. Goldstock taught his students that the most important thing a writer needs is peace, quiet, an empty room. "Emotion recollected in tranquility," he said, quoting Wordsworth. The other things a writer needed were something to write on and something to write with, that was all.

I told Mr. Goldstock of my problems with the speed by which I had to learn English in the seventh grade, when I arrived in the United States from Spain. I had to learn the language because the teachers realized that I would never learn it in ESL classes, seeing how all I did around other children was misbehave. Also, on the playground I had to learn it in order to defend myself against bullies. I learned the language so fast (six, seven months) that I wasn't sure I could do anything with it. I still remember writing "Sherman" instead of "Chairman" (Mao) on one paper. I still made the mistake of confusing "there" and "their" and "they're," and "to" and "too." It was a slow process, but in Goldstock's class, my writing improved.

One of the assignments I remember best was the ending we had to invent to Frank Stockton's "The Lady or The Tiger." It was in Mr. Goldstock's class that I switched from thinking about writing in Spanish to thinking about writing in English. English was the language of Poe's "The Raven," Hawthorne's "Rapaccini's Daughter," Melville's "Bartleby The Scrivener," Flannery O'connor's "A Good Man is Hard to Find" and "Parker's Back," and Joyce Carol Oates' "How I Contemplated The World . . . ," whose stories taught me that you can be not only creative with language but with form. I was also introduced to the work of Langston Hughes, Richard Wright, James Baldwin. I still remember the sound of Gwendolyn Brooks' "We Be Cool."

Joel Goldstock was patient with my mistakes—bless him. Though he had a full class of twenty-five to twenty-eight students, he took his time with me. Not that he saw anything special in my ability, any more than what he saw in his other students, but everything he said clicked in me. He brought his own work and shared it with us. For me, it was an important lesson about teaching that I would remember later, and one that has come in handy over the years. As a teacher, my own students love it when I tell them I too will do the assignment, just as a warm up. If I can do it, I tell them, so can they. We share the beauty of English, and my job is to prop myself up as an example to them. My job is to make them proud of this beautiful language they were born into, but somehow come to take for granted.

The door to the world of English and literature was wide open, and I had already taken my first steps. English was Holden Caulfield in Salinger's *The Catcher in The Rye,* Saul Bellow's *Seize the Day*, James Baldwin's *Sonny's Blues* and I learned from all these books the idea of setting, tone, and characterization. Certainly I was also learning the importance of writing about where one comes from. It was already a familiar question to me.

Mr. Goldstock, the collector of stuff, brought us objects to look at. Artifacts from wars, ships, planes—he approached the teaching of writing like an artist teaches his/her students about the importance of sketching still lifes. "Look and see,"

Virgil Suárez

he said. "Look hard and see hard. When you get tired of looking, look some more."

Of course, these were lessons I thought I had already
learned from my grandmother, but in Mr. Alvarado's and Mr.
Goldstock's classes, I was exposed to these same ideas in English in this new country where I was to continue being an
exile, where my accent, my awkward, foreign ways would
always give away where I was from. The question was and is
always presented to me: "where are you from?" The reply
(though it has caused me some trouble) is always the same.
Cuba, the land—whether reconstructed in my memory and
recreated on film—that runs in my veins.

III.

In 1980 I graduated from Huntington Park Senior High
School in the Los Angeles Unified School District and went to
college at California State University at Long Beach. There I
was once again lucky. I was entertaining the idea of becoming
a painter or going into journalism when I met Elliot Fried,
who asked "Where you from?" I had learned not to say "Cuba"
so fast—that answer had given a black eye and a couple of
busted lips back in school. I told him what city in Los Angeles,
and he said, "No, country. I detect an accent."

Ah, the accent. So I gave in and told him I was Cuban.
"Have you ever thought about writing about where you come
from," he said. "I'm teaching a novel-writing workshop, and if
you're interested." The rest is my personal history, as they
say. I enrolled in Professor Fried's novel-writing workshop
and answered his question by writing *The Cutter,* my first
novel written, second published. Elliot Fried made writing not
only a life style, but for the one year I wrote my novel, an
addiction. As I wrote about one character, one setting, one
year in the life of my character, one overwhelming question,
he taught me that this was the material.

Writing about Cuban-Americans and Cuban-American life was enough. There would be no other subject matter more compelling for me.

Though I had learned much under Joel Goldstock, I still didn't know how to write a sentence in English to save my life, but Elliot Fried inspired me to keep going. He taught me the essentials: dedication and discipline. I wrote in the morning, the afternoon, at night—I wrote all the time. Within the year I had finished the first draft of the novel. Elliot said he was impressed. He said I was the first student to ever do such a thing in any of his classes.

I was hooked. I couldn't stop writing poems, short stories, my novel. Elliot Fried introduced his students to the "life" of the writer. How to live well and write well. My sentences got better. Elliot pointed out the first sentence he liked early in the fourth chapter of The Cutter, which was "The raindrops that hang from the top of the braided wires fall when the chickens peck on the sides of the cage." He showed me how images work and the "payoff" they offer the reader.

The second important element of Elliot Fried's teaching was that he inspired his students to keep reading. Read contemporary authors. In my case, he recommended I go to the library and look at the work of other Cuban-American writers. I didn't know in 1980 if there would be any (at least at the California State University, at Long Beach library, I found none), but I did go to the library and found Cuban literature in translation, specifically the work of Guillermo Cabrera Infante, Lydia Cabrera, Jose Lezama Lima, Virgilio Piñero, and later in 1982-83, Reinaldo Arenas' El central, which had a profound effect on me, and The Cutter. It was a gold mine I struck. I took home books by the crateful.

I didn't find a single book by Cuban-American writers, and I wasn't sure I knew what that meant. I did find, however, the work of Jose Antonio Villarreal and Rudolfo Anaya, two Chicano authors who've inspired me all through the years. Both Pocho and Bless Me, Ultima speak directly about the essence of what it means to by hyphenated-American. With these two books I began to see the kind of shape my work would have to take if I was to consider myself, or be considered by others, a Cuban-American writer.

In the four years I spent studying with Elliot Fried at California State University at Long Beach, I learned more than at any other time in my life. By the time I graduated I had written so much, but nothing had yet seen the light of print. Elliot had stressed the work more than publication, which is always a good thing for a beginning writer. In 1984, he encouraged me to apply to graduate school and leave California because, for one thing, I couldn't stay at Long Beach because the Masters of Fine Arts program would be ten more years in coming.

"See this big beautiful country," Elliot told me, and once again I heeded his advice.

I applied to the University of California at Irvine and the University of Oregon and a couple of others I can't remember, and they all turned me down except for the University of Arizona. So I entered the Masters of Fine Arts program in Creative Writing. I worked with two people at Arizona, whom, I learned later, had been instrumental in my having been accepted. They turned away from both my GRE scores and GPA and focused on the strengths of my writing. They liked the writing samples I had sent them from *The Cutter*. Both Robert Houston and later Vance Bourjaily would help me revise that book and challenged me to send it out to editors and agents in New York. They, too, delighted in my love of Latin American literature, specially the literature of Cuba and Mexico.

"I want to become a Cuban-American writer," I said to them.

"Become a writing fool and you just might," they said.

I worked hard at my writing. Robert Houston and Vance Bourjaily shaved about ten years from my apprenticeship as a writer. They took me and read my work carefully, and helped me see all the specific things I was doing wrong. Like Elliot Fried, they took time out from their own work to read my work and help me. Another important lesson about teaching I have never forgotten. In order to receive: give!

When Vance Bourjaily accepted the position to run the creative writing program at Louisiana State University, I was ready to move with him. There I became Vance Bourjaily's administrative assistant, a job that has taught me much about the behind-the-scenes running of a creative writing program, but it also offered me the continuity of working one-on-one with Vance.

After work, I wrote, and what I wrote I showed to him. By 1987, I had finished the final draft of *The Cutter,* and had stared to work on this other novel titled *Latin Jazz.* This was a novel inspired by the 1980 Mariel Boatlift Exodus which brought well over one hundred thousand Cubans to South Florida. It was also a novel inspired by Luis Navarro Rubio, my friend's grandfather and surrogate grandfather to me in Los Angeles (*Latin Jazz* is dedicated to him and his memory, and so much of it is *him*).

The Mariel Boatlift captured my imagination like no other event, so I wrote the novel, trying to keep up with everything that was happening. Having worked on *The Cutter,* I didn't know that my next book would be about Cuban-Americans, but that's exactly what I though of *Latin Jazz.* Whereas *The Cutter* helped me find an agent in New York, *Latin Jazz* broke into the light of print by 1989. It was hailed as the first Cuban-American novel to be published by a major New York publishing house, but that is not true. By 1989, there was an explosion of publishing about the Cuban-American experience. Elias Miguel Muñoz had published *Crazy Love* and Roberto G. Fernández *Raining Backwards*, both excellent novels about Cubans on this side of exile. A few months after *Latin Jazz* was published, Oscar Hijuelos published *The Mambo Kings Play Songs of Love*, which won the Pulitzer Prize and helped put the spotlight on all writing from and

Virgil Suárez

about Latinos/as in the United States. In 1983 he had written a wonderful novel called *Our House in the Last World,* which back then I didn't know existed because the California State University at Long Beach library didn't have it.

Today there is so much good writing about the Cuban-American experience that it is hard to keep up with all of it, but I try. I try because I know that it is likely to keep growing, being nurtured by so many wonderful practitioners, growing in the dazzling garden that is American Literature.

IV.

After word. There comes a time in every writer's creative life, when he or she must face the solitude of the work, work done away from teachers and mentors. I graduated from Louisiana State University in the spring of 1987. Though I've kept in touch with Vance and all the other mentors, except those in high school (I still ask a friend once in a while about Alvarado—I hear he's retired), I set out that year to write, write more about what I knew I had been taught. I moved to Miami, met my wife, started several novels, completed drafts of *Havana Thursdays* and *Going Under,* both published recently, had a child, taught high school, moved back to Baton Rouge to teach as an instructor at Louisiana State University, left when they didn't want to hire me with benefits and a chance at tenure (by then I think I had four books out and another daughter, had become interested too in breeding and showing canaries—more on that later), and Florida State University which saved me and my family from many desperate days, and then, just when I thought I had been through with any kind of apprenticeship with mentors, along came Jerome H. Stern.

I cannot hide my feelings for Jerry as teacher, friend, fellow writer, and, yes, mentor. Jerry taught me—at a time when my creativity ebbed at an all-time low (all right, I suffered writer's block when I first arrived)—how to love writing again. Not only through his wonderfully witty and incisive book, *Making Shapely Fiction*, which I have used in every one of my writing classes since I got here, but by being there in the same hallways, committee meetings, offices, and lunches. Whenever I needed him, Jerry was always there.

Jerome Stern loved the power of the word, and he let everyone know it. He loved writing, no matter what form it took—all he asked was that it had passion, feeling, that it was engaging and good. Jerry got me writing again about my past. Through the challenge of his 250 word micro-fictions, he got me writing about some stuff I never thought I would write about, mainly about some memories of my childhood in Havana. It seemed that with every year since I had started teaching at Florida State University, Jerry and I got closer. He enjoyed talking shop. Actually, he loved it. What students were good in my classes. What books I was reading. Having my students read. I keep in mind the twenty-eight years he had put into the teaching of writing. He possessed the aura of someone who loved every minute of those twenty-eight years.

He turned me on to the idea that if you get the right chemistry in the class, and you get them energized and moti-vated, then the students themselves would give me back the gift and the magic; they'd give me back the essence of the joy of writing within a community of people doing the same thing, encouraging each other, proving to each other that writing, yes, is a lonely endeavor, but then there is all that human interaction—at the bottom or rather end of it, human commu-nication. It was an important lesson I had overlooked in all my years as a student, being so selfish and needy.

Now I knew the importance of this exchange. Writing and writing workshops are the perfect excuse to come into contact with other people, and then love what happens. The magic is there, and Jerry was a natural at tapping it. Mining it. Jerry was the only person to ever step into my bird room and not look at me and say "you're crazy, what's this with all these birds?" Instead he stood for a moment, looked and me and

Virgil Suárez

smiled and said "tell me more about this, how interesting." He knew these canaries and my new life as a canaryculturist would one day lead to new material. Jerry had a wonderful intuition about what kinds of stories people needed to tell. We also shared a like for William Wharton's classic novel *Birdy*.

Every time I asked Jerry to visit my classes and talk, he came in and charmed not only the students, but the teacher as well. I couldn't believe how easy he made the teaching of writing seem. He knew how to entertain, how to engage the mind. So sharp was his wit, so quick was he at illustrating his points with examples, that I quickly realized that he possessed a gift and talent I wanted to have. Jerry knew how to spot talent in the student and then feed that talent so that it grew hungrier. I know so many times I came so close to asking him to let me sit in in his own workshops.

I wanted to tap into that gift, but also through Jerry's teachings become a better teacher myself. He had written what I believe to be the most insightful and funny book about writing, and I now wanted to learn it by memory. This was Jerry's bag of goodies, and I wanted to dig in with both hands.

Like with his students, Jerry encouraged only the best in me. With my writing, with my teaching, and living as good and dignified a life as possible. For all of this I will always be grateful to him and he will always be in my memory. *En paz descanse*. Rest in peace, friend.

And memory, as I find myself once again back on track with the word (I have started work on my canary novel), is the one tool by which I can preserve the voices and pay homage to the people who've given me so much of the fire to light my imagination on such a stormy and cold journey as is being a writer from two cultures, two worlds.

The Mystery of Closed Doors

What went on behind the closed door that kept me from seeing my sick grandmother became obvious through another woman who lived in the hostel where we first lived in Madrid. Mariana, the old woman, and her daughter (whose name I no longer remember) shared the room at the end of the hallway. In the evening, her daughter helped Mariana walk into the common living room where there was a radio and a large window through which one could view the city. The old woman, well into senility, sat on the worn sofa and mumbled to herself. At first I thought she was praying, but I learned fast that she was out of her mind. Her daughter sat across from her to make sure that Mariana wouldn't lift up her skirt or open her blouse. I was attracted to this scene because Mariana, of course, reminded me so much of my grandmother. Mariana's daughter and my mother became friends. Often, they sat together and spoke of their lives in Havana. I sat with them, too, and I watched Mariana's eyes for some sense of recognition. The following spring Mariana became bedridden, having fallen and broken her hip.

I had already started school in Spain and, as had been the case in Cuba, I quickly was singled out as an outsider because of my accent. In Cuba it had been because of my parents' dissent toward the revolution. I think this was the beginning of my accepting my position as a foreigner and exile everywhere I went and lived. I am comfortable with the idea of being the outsider; I embrace this fact now because it is what fuels my creativity, and because I have learned to live without the need of human contact outside family and close friends. Anyway, one afternoon after I had returned from school, I was going into my parents' room when I noticed the open door down the hall. Approaching slowly, I pushed the door and Mariana's daughter did not greet me there as I had expected. Instead, I found old Mariana on her bed naked to the waist. Her legs were spread and there was this brown stuff all over her thighs, pubis and stomach. Then the smell hit me, and I understood what the stuff was: human feces. *"QUÉ HACES?"* the voice said from behind me. It was Mariana's daughter coming down the hallway with a pail of water and several towels over her shoulder. "Get out of here," she said. "You shouldn't see this." I stood there despite what she was saying. "My mother is sick," she said. "Can't you see? She needs to be left alone. In peace. GET OUT!" I left the room and quickly went to my parents' room. Later, after Mariana's daughter told my mother what I had done, my mother sat with me and explained as best as she could about the "little accidents" people have in their old age. "Was this what happened to Mima?" I asked. Answers are always so slow in coming.

American Sidewalk

Sunday mornings
church rush
summer sales
leftovers in garage sales
kids who spit tasteless gum
& the stranger who walks
by and gets it stuck
on his shoes

heavy tumult
the litter
is not in its place
the pigeons
tinged with exhaust
fly by or hover
leaving their landmarks

broken glass
cigarette butts
crushed soda cans
& the brown paper
are all part of you
night's prelude

& the slow falling
gentle cool dew
renders you tired
monday morning
at last

rest for a while
before the sweepers
arrive with their
steel brushes

Virgil Suárez

No Nocturne for the Ravaged

for Leroy V. Quintana

I. *First Day of School at Henry T. Gage*
Junior High School

I arrived in the clothes of a fool: denim jacket & matching bell-bottom pants, a long-sleeved shirt buttoned at the neck. First period was 4th Period Physical Education. The last 10 minutes: shower time. I walked into the penumbra of the gym office where I was told in the bark of this new foreign tongue that I was to take a shower. I pleaded to no avail. I was clean. I was crisp. I was in no condition to shower. No luck. I was led to the ammonia saturated lockers & showers, & though I didn't yet speak English I was made to go naked into the showers, naked in front of hundreds of boys, and broken into this idea of nakedness. For everybody this was business as usual. They stood around, carousing as they spat on & pissed & snapped towels at each other. Their howls echoed high above, caught in the I-beam ceiling. I walked naked in front of so many eyes who'd never seen one so weak & frail of spirit. I took the fastest shower of my life, sidestepped the towel dispenser & as I walked past a trash can, I slipped & fell—I heard the roar of laughter—& cut the back of my head open. This was the mark, my mark, that I was to wear for the rest of my public school education.

Virgil Suárez

II. *Marijuana David*

who spoke words even foreign to the Spanish I spoke
    when he said *"Mota"* & *"Leño"* & *"Marijuana."*
I shrugged, not understanding. He said, "I've got
    some, ese."
    "Whatever you need, *carnal*. I've got it."
Years later, this same boy, with a name now,
    a face gone soft to sniffed glue & punches
took a knife to the stomach during lunch—
    I had received mine long ago through the heart.

III. *The Wasabi Connection*

Befriended a lifelong philosopher kindred spirit of the
    absurd.
In his new made-up name (I christened him) Wasabi
    Kanastoga
& I sat in Mr. K's eighth-grade science class &
    watched as Mr. K
fondled the 9th-grade/cheerleader/assistant behind
    the counter
of microscopes, beakers, & vials. Mr. K, who caught
    us looking,
called us into his office and asked us what we
    thought it was we
were looking at. We shook our heads no and said
    nothing. Mr. K
made us spit out our gums into a big jar at the bot-
    tom of which
there were other gums, gone green with fungus, from
    all those
in class who knew of Mr. K's weakness of mind and
    spirit.

Virgil Suárez

IV. *Dolores*

better known as La Gata de La Trece
sat between Wasabi & I in Mr. K's class
she cared as much for science as we did
Wasabi constantly staring at her exposed
belly button, soft skin pinched by the tight
belt & chords we loved what we
could never possess Dolores
with the most beautiful belly button
we'd ever laid eyes on then one
day she caught us looking & she slapped
us threatened us with the fear
of her homeboys "You'll see," she told us,
"My homeboys'll kick your ass."
& so we took our chances & dared look again

V. *Hopeful The Fear Made Us Vanish*

With those years of the endless half-burnt
burritos, soggy grilled cheeses,
     jello puddings, there were also the moments
of terror waiting for the homeboys,
all the little gangsters, to kick our asses.
     Expecting the worst, we snuck out of school
as soon as the last bell rang, hoping we got lost
in the nearly twenty-five hundred faces,
     praying we'd become experts at the art of blending in.
We ran out beyond the fenced entrances
to meet our rides, and always made it to the safety
     of adult supervision & familiar faces out of breath,
scared shitless, drenched in sweat, always hopeful
the fear made us vanish.

Virgil Suárez

VI.   *The Errand Boy*

Runner of love errands
between a Miss C
& a Mr. S, each married

to other people.
Who knows what
those love notes

said? I imagined
they spelled out
some kind of love.

I remember
so many of them,
perfumed, neatly folded,

all hid the best-kept
of school secrets—
I always the deliverer

of such good news.

VII. *Mr. Filbin*

The Drafting teacher—
thin as a pencil & unsteady
with his eyes & hands.
In his class, we'd ask
"Hey, Mr. Filbin, what do you know?"
& he'd say, nodding, "Nothing,
I know nothing. Don't know."
Some vato threatened
us because we whistled
"Three Blind Mice."
Apparently it was the *trucha*
call for his gang.
What did we know?

Virgil Suárez

VIII. *Little Mosca*

Shared gym lockers with Marcos, the ruffian (may
you be locked away now for good). We, the helpless &
the innocent, knew you as The Terrorist, because you
inflicted the idea of hopelessness & violence into our
lives. Marcos smelled of hard-boiled eggs. His favorite
pastime was thrusting his ass up against our faces &
farting. He spat on us, too. "Loogie alert!" he
screamed & spat. He scratched his ass, then rubbed
his fingers under our noses. He wasn't any taller
than the rest of us. Any stronger. But he belonged to
a gang & so none of us dared touch him. He sure
knew how to work us into a frenzy of hate & fear.
Our worst days, which were many, was when he
showed up to class. We prayed for his sickness, for
him to play hooky, go sniff glue, smoke pot or screw
girls like he said he did all the time. We didn't care.
Mostly we hoped for the police to put him away, for
good—anything was better than having to deal with
this unholy terror. How you made us suffer, you
nasty son of a bitch. Wherever you are now, this is to
let you know of our resentment.

IX. *First Love*

Tana B—my first love.
She was blond & beautiful

& she'd have nothing
 to do with me, the wetback,

freshly arrived immigrant.
 To her we, all of us brown people,

 were from Tijuana. She let the word
hiss out of her mouth. I loved her

 nonetheless, learned to love her
the way a foreigner loves America

with a bittersweet pain/pang
 of hate love.

Virgil Suárez

X. *English As A Second Language*

Learned it fast.
Had to, for this
was to be the language
of survival. Knew
I had to learn it
when I squirted
ink on Watkins & Tommy
Laveer's Hawaiian shirts.
They chased me around,
cornered me & beat me up—
all along I tried to explain.
They told me to speak English,
that if I didn't they'd rip my tongue
out of my mouth. & so I learned
it, learned it in six months,
& English would never
again sound like the bark of mad dogs.

Flash Flesh

When we moved from Miami to Los Angeles, we lived in an apartment building on Marbrisa Street, across from a McDonald's. One day I was sitting on the front stairs of the building, waiting for Julio, my Nicaraguan friend, to get home so we could play catch. The stairs was my favorite spot for sitting and looking out at the street. Nothing new was happening, just the usual: women sweeping leaves and dust off their porches, men working under the hoods of their cars.

I sat there gripping and shaping the McGregor glove my father had bought for me at Thrifty's. It would take a while to break in the new leather. Then, out of nowhere, it seemed, a *vato* or *pachuco*, as the people who knew them in the neighborhood called them, came walking down the sidewalk, arm-in-arm with his girlfriend.

It was Sunday, so they were sporting their best clothes: he with crisply creased chinos, a Pendleton shirt buttoned to the collar, a sparkling belt buckle and shiny black shoes; she with a white, low-cut blouse too short to cover her belly button, cords and white sandals.

She also wore so much make-up and eye shadow that her face looked like a mask. Her hair stood in a curl over her pale forehead, the rest of it spilling over her brown shoulders and the front of her big breasts. Her corduroy pants were tight, even tighter in the crotch, so tight I thought of my hand in my glove and how the leather stitches welted against my fingers.

The *vato*, seeing me eyeing him and his girlfriend, walked up to the stairs where I sat and said, "Hey, ese, where you from?"

"Cuba," I said.

"A *Cuba-Cubanito*," he said, and turned to the young woman. "This is my ruca, say hello."

"Hello, Ruca," I said, not knowing that *ruca* meant girlfriend.

"Ruca's not my name," she said.

"She's *La Lupe de la Trece, ese*," he said, reaching into his shirt pocket, from which he withdrew a pack of Marlboros. "You want one?" he said, and tapped out a cigarette."

"I don't smoke," I said, and placed the glove on the step between my legs.

"Umm," he said, and lit his cigarette. He acted real suave and let the smoke swirl around his face. He blew the rest in front of me.

It was then I noticed the tear tatoo under his right eye and *"La Vida Loca"* written out in script on his neck. "What you looking at, *ese*?" he said.

"Nothing," I told him.

"Hey, *pendejo*, how old are you?"

"He's a kid," she said.

"Twelve," I answered.

"Twelve," he said, and laughed. "That's old enough."

I should have stood up then and gone upstairs to a world more familiar to me, but I kept staring at the woman's breasts, at the V of her cleavage and the soft skin there.

Spared Angola

"You have any money?" he asked.

"No."

"Can you get some?"

"What for?" That was the wrong question.

"What for? What for?" he said, then. "Are you insulting my girl, eh?"

"No," I said.

"If you get a ten," he said, and stopped to put his hand on her breast, "she'll show you something."

"Cut it out," she said, getting his hand away from her breast.

"With, *mira*," he said, and rubbed the tip of his fingers, "with ten dollars, you can see her *panocha*."

Panocha. I didn't know what that was, but it was clear that it was some part of her anatomy.

I kept hoping someone would come to the rescue, like Julio, but no one did. I was alone on this one.

He started to grab the woman, and she kept fending him off. I didn't know how these two could be together, but something kept my attention. He pawed at her flesh, of which I was seeing some.

In one attempt, he pulled down her blouse and grabbed one of her breasts. "See this," he said, and smiled. "You see this mark right here."

I looked at her flesh. I saw the brown pink of her nipple, then the hickie he pointed to. "I gave her this," he said.

I looked on.

"Stop it, *no chingues*," she said, slipping her breast back inside her blouse.

"Okay, *ese*," he said. "You can have her if you give me your glove."

I told him I couldn't do it, my father would kill me.

"INSULT NUMBER THREE," he shouted. "Shit. You keep offending my woman."

I put my foot on the glove.

Virgil Suárez

"¡Horale! Okay," he said. "Tell you what, if you give me the glove, she'll let you see her *panocha*."

He worked furiously at unbuckling her belt, the cigarette dangling from the corner of his mouth, a strand of his slick hair falling over his eyes.

I was speechless. I didn't know whether to run or shout for help. When he couldn't do it, her pants being too tight, he shoved his hand inside her pants and grabbed her crotch. She screamed and started to hit him with her fists. Suddenly he pulled his hand out. He presented his closed hand to me. "Look here," he said, opening his fingers one by one.

In between his fingers were curly pubic hairs. He picked them one by one and threw them at my face. *"Pendejos, pendejos, pendejos,"* he said. "Perfumed pubic hair. How about it, *pinche cabrón?"*

"Let's go, Victor," she said. "Leave him alone and let's go."

"No," he said. "Can't you see it in his eyes. He likes you."

Victor brought his fingers close to my face again. I froze. With one hand on my shoulder, the hand with the cigarette—I feared he would burn my ears—he held my attention and touched the tip of my nose with the fingers of the other hand. He rubbed the smell, *her scent,* under my nostril, then touched the tip of my nose. I pulled my head back and he let go. He was smiling, and I could see the pink of his tongue behind his dirty teeth.

"Okay, but let's get out of here," she said.

"No, last deal, my friend," he said. Once he was done smoking, he flicked the butt on the ground and crushed it out with his shoe. The gutted cigarette on the sidewalk blew away with a gust of wind.

"For your glove," he said, "she will pull on your slinky."

"No, *ya vámonos,*" she said.

"How about it, *Cubanito pendejito?*"

"Gotta go," I said, and stood up.

He tried to grab the glove off my hand, but I was quicker than he was. Then, my moving up the stairs with the glove upset him.

"¡Horale cabrón," he said. "Don't let me catch you around here anymore or I'll kick your ass. If not me, then one of my homeboys."

I walked up and stopped at the top of the stairs, turned and looked down one more time. He was saying, ". . . insulted my ruca and I don't like that. Nobody insults *La Lupe de la Trece* and gets away with it."

I left them both there and hurried to my apartment, opened the door, put the glove down on the sofa and closed the door behind me. My mother was sewing in the bedroom; my father was napping on the easy chair.

I went to the bathroom and stood by the sink. I closed my eyes and thought of the girl and her flesh. The sweet scent of the perfume came up through my nose, a little faint. Flesh. Soft and brown. Her flesh. Pink nipples. The contour of her belly button, the fuzzy hairs there. Her crotch. I looked into the medicine cabinet mirror and saw my own adolescent face. Punk, I thought. I felt embarrassed and humiliated, and yet excited. Extremely excited at the nagging smell rising in through my nostrils.

I was twelve. I thought about how much longer it would be before I became acquainted with the flesh of a woman.

Virgil Suárez

Lucha Libre

When we lived in the Spanish Arms Apartments off Marbrisa Avenue, next to the McDonalds in Huntington Park, California, my parents decided they wanted to learn to speak English. "Learn to defend ourselves," that's how my father put it. This was around 1974 or 1975, and by then he had already had a few showdowns with Mexican-Americans or "pochos" who didn't want to speak Spanish. It drove my father into rages. "How could you not know Spanish," he would say, pointing at their name tags. "Look where you come from." The young men and women would merely look at him as though he were mad. Anyway, they decided to go to night school at the local elementary and pick up a few words, enough to fend for themselves on the streets. These classes were offered between six and eight every night, Monday through Thursday, and it made the schedule pretty tough on my parents. By this time my mother was not working in the same factory as my father, so he had to punch the clock out and then zoom over and pick her up.

They made an arrangement with a couple of friends of theirs to keep an eye on me after I came home from school. So, for the first few weeks that they were taking classes, I sat in the living room of Hilda and Rey's house and watched television. Usually I would watch the cartoons, like "Johnny Quest" and "Speed Racer." But then Rey would himself get home from work and he wanted to watch *Lucha Libre* on KMEX, Channel 34. He was the one who got me hooked into watching wrestling because he said it was all action, and that it was true: those guys did hurt themselves pretty badly.

🐢 🐢 🐢

I don't know if *Lucha Libre* was on every day in the afternoon or only on Wednesday, but every week that passed I liked it more and more and came around to look forward to it, so much so that on the particular days, I couldn't wait to get home from school so I could watch it. A lot of people say that the mid-70s were the Golden Age of *Lucha Libre*. I would agree. Those guys really knew how to put on a show.

🐢 🐢 🐢

Rey and I would sit in the living room and watch the action from the Los Angeles Olympic Auditorium. We sat around and drank sodas and munched on saltine crackers and watched. "That's all true," Rey would often turn to me and say. I was caught in the magic of the violence. I sat there and stared, looking for ways that these men would give their craft away. I mean, how could they hit themselves so hard, coming off the ropes, then get up and continue to slug it out a few seconds later. Rey liked it when it was tag-team wrestling and the guys losing would keep getting tossed out of the ring. I preferred when the bad guys got caught in the corner, then

Virgil Suárez

later pinned and the referee would slam his hand down three times and the bell would signal the end of the match.

🐢 🐢 🐢

So many months passed by with us watching *Lucha Libre*. Rey and I bet on the winning teams. Of course, we didn't bet real money, but we bet anyway, just to see who could pick the winning teams. My other favorite moments were after the fights, when these sweaty, saliva-frothing, out-of-breath men would approach the host with the microphone, and they would try to intimidate him. I only remember the name of my favorite host: Jaime Jarrin. He always shivered when guys like André the Giant stood next to him, and even though André was on the good-guys' team, Jaime tried to keep his distance.

🐢 🐢 🐢

There was and still is, of course, something regal about wrestling, but the old days with Johnny Chibuye, André the Giant, Greg Valentine and John Toulous and his famous corkscrew were the best. When those guys charged up into the ring, the crowd roared. Rey and I shifted in our seats. We got ready for the heavy-duty hitting action.

🐢 🐢 🐢

My parents stopped going to school to learn English; they got tired from the hectic schedules and running around. It was a time when my mother didn't know how to drive and she had to rely on my father to pick her up and take her to the places she wanted to go. So when they stopped going to school, my afternoon, over at Rey and Hilda's came to an end.

🐢 🐢 🐢

Luckily, *Lucha Libre* was moved to Saturday morning when I could spend the entire Saturday morning watching in my room, still in my pajamas. Ah, those were glorious mornings. It didn't bother my parents that I would watch television all day, practically. What was an only son to do, but find ways of to entertain himself, and there was no better entertainment than *Lucha Libre* for a boy of thirteen on the verge of a major voice change, on the verge of hair, on the verge of his manhood.

Virgil Suárez

Milagros *La Flaca*

Was the first girl I ever made out with.
She was all skin and bones. Wore
orthodontic braces, which while we kissed
and fondled that day in the garage,
    cut up my lips real bad.

Her pelvis dug into my waist as we ground
into pleasure. She refused to let me touch
her under her blouse. We were thirteen.
The way she kissed, I thought, had something
    to do with her name: miracle.

She got me in trouble for the first time
with the law. I visited her house on Saturdays,
after her parents left to work the flea markets.
She never let me inside the house
    out of respect for her parents.

I waited for her in the garage. Each Saturday
I got there earlier. One time I was there so early
after her parents had left, that the next-door
neighbor saw me and called the cops.
    They came, asked me a few questions,

and since I wouldn't cooperate with the right
answers, they took me in. There were two of them,
and they wouldn't talk to each other as they drove
me to the station. I asked what I had done wrong.
    They drove and kept quiet.

Spared Angola　　　　　　　　🐢 115

But I insisted upon answers, until the one driving
looked up at the rearview mirror and shouted to shut
the fuck up, and so I did, for a while, until I started
to tell them about what I was doing in the garage.
  We drove into the parking lot behind the station.

The cop who wasn't driving and who hadn't said a word,
came around the side of the car, opened my door,
reach in, and pulled me out by the hair. He choked
me and left me breathless for a few moments.
  "When we say 'shut up,'" he said, "we mean it."

And so I didn't talk after that. They called my parents.
They came to pick me up at the station. The chief of
police assured my father this wouldn't go on record.
They shook hands. On the way home, my mother cried,
  and my father refused to talk.

As soon as we got home, I tried to explain
what happened. My mother said Milagros,
was no good for me, no good indeed if she
was already getting me into trouble with the law.
  I was not to see her again.

Next Saturday, I didn't go see her. I didn't call.
Neither did she. Soon we forgot about each other.
I tried to anyway, until I saw us necking in the garage,
her braces cut my already cut and raw lips,
  the taste of her tongue in my mouth,
    remnants now of a girl named Milagros.

Virgil Suárez

1965 Dodge Dart

My father paid $500 for it in 1974
when we first arrived in the U.S.
from Spain. Though not in the best
of shape, it was the biggest &
grandest thing we'd ever owned.

It took my mother to work, me
to school & my father off to the factory
where he cut patterns for blue jeans
& denim skirts. The car lasted ten
more years, my father nursing it back

each time it broke & it became the car
I drove to school to impress the girls,
who laughed & giggled at so much
lack-luster chrome & rusted metal.
The Dart was no match for a Mustang

or Camaro, or some other muscle car
the hip students drove in those days
of vanity & foolishness. Even when
we could afford to, my father refused
to sell the Dodge. Like me, he hung

on to the familiar musk of the worn
& cracked leather of the seats
& dashboard, the feel of the beat-up
interior. "Women don't understand
these things," my father'd say when

my mother told him to get rid of the piece
of junk—that Dart was junkyard-bound
& my father & I were trying hard.
A lot of money would have to be sunk
into it before it looked like new—what

price for memories? Mine in youth.
The back seat of that car became
the place where I first experienced
the pleasures & perils of women.
Yes, it was our car, the only one

we had for a decade in Los Angeles, CA.
A simple machine, that taught me years
later, as a consumer in an age of techno-info
gone awry, that a car, if it is to bring
you peace of mind & be dependable,

must be easy to repair. Hood popped
open, you should be able to look
past the engine & see the ground.
Anything else clutters & confuses:
wires, fuel injection, computers . . .

Finally in 1984 when I went away
to school, my father sold the Dart.
I got drunk that same night
because it was a kind of passing,
a kind of death. "It is in good hands,"

Virgil Suárez

my father assured me on the line
from L. A. to Tucson, Arizona.
My father said he sold the car
to his friend Earl, whom he called
"El Ro." An American friend

with whom he worked at the furniture
packaging warehouse. "He'll take
good care of it." No matter, I thought.
Earl paid my father $600 for the Dart.
"Funny," said my old man. "After

all the years, we make a profit."
We never had reason to engage
in small talk, my father & I, less
after he sold the car. Sometimes
when I think of that 1965 Dodge Dart,

I still see myself behind the wheel,
hands steady, head held high,
I am driving in slow motion down
so many countless, uncertain
and perilous American roads.

Just Talk

Father says the birds in Mexico City fall amid flight from the polluted skies. They fall from the trees in the parks. On the sidewalks. We talk about the situation all over Latin America. Sendero Luminoso in Peru massacres innocent people, even the Indians. Guatemala, too, suffers from guerrilla havoc. And those cocaine wheelers and dealers in Columbia and Bolivia. And let's not forget the macho dictators who know the secrets of power longevity, who know how to break down the opposition by crushing their families first: Castro in Cuba (always Castro in Cuba . . .), Pinochet in Chile, Somoza in Nicaragua, Noriega in Panama. And take Argentina, for example. For a president they have a smooth talker with funny-looking sideburns; he looks like a tango dancer straight out of the ballroom. Things are bad, father says, everywhere. Be thankful to live here in the USA. My turn comes and I think of all the hatred & violence on the streets. The way people die quickly in 8-to-5 jobs, like Thoreau said, living lives of quiet desperation . . . . Father gives me his best you're-full-of-shit look. I may not know what I'm talking about, but I know what I see and I don't like it. Being ill at ease with poorly chosen words, I try to make my point. I say . . . I say, daily here in the great *El Norte*, I witness people's souls rot like uneaten fruit and they, too, fall to the earth, yeah, like those birds in Mexico City. Some shrivel up slowly and, sure, okay, people die all over the world. Young. Because of wars. Starvation. Over God. And sure, okay, unnatural causes, but here in the good old US of A they wilt, wilt I say, and die slow painful humiliating deaths. I tell my father, I say, I saw this old lady in a Melrose convalescent home. Yes, some son or daughter must have put her in there. It was past midnight and she was slumped over asleep on the sofa of the lobby in front of this big window whose sign read WE TAKE CARE OF YOUR LOVED ONES. Father says, he says, what's your point, son? I say, I tell him, hell, the best we can hope for here is that when our turn comes to drop dead that a hungry crow or mockingbird finds us and pecks out our hearts first.

Half Time

How much longer, father,
until the bays of your hairline
   become oceans of skin
on your forehead? When your hair
         falls & you'll have to wipe

      the sweat from your brow
with a handkerchief—
   yet more things to carry, to worry about.
You old immigrant. Refugee.
      Out of your passion

      I sprang forth to witness
you come & go from the house
   in Havana you bought
on your policeman's salary,
         when the daily work got rough,

      rougher than you'd imagine.
Twice I listened, twice,
   when you'd scream because madness
then, like now, was possible.
         That same scream brought us here,

      to this new land. I remember too
that in Madrid you fell on the floor
   & I ran down the apartment hallways
in my underwear like a creature stirred
         in the night, frightened & scared

Virgil Suárez

wild-eyed, something went wrong.
But your heart kick-started once more,
   after the CPR & the familial tenderness,
for to have lost you, well . . .
     Now here we are,

     more than twenty years later
well into your half-time.
   It is true: one doesn't get any younger,
one doesn't learn new tricks
     & the years keep gnawing.

     I still watch you come & go,
& from the distance of five hundred miles
   some of your advice,
balled-up truths like *"¡Los golpes enseñan!"*
     "¡Cuando el mar está de cagar,

     no valen guayabas verdes!"
still make my ears ring.

Spared Angola

Animalia

As a child the games to break boredom included a certain cruelty. Plucked wings from flies, caught lizards and gheckos, trapped fireflies in jars. I kept my distance from the frogs, which the other kids in the neighborhood, aware of my terror, insisted in putting down the back of my shirt or pants. We caught lizards with long grass stems and noosed them around their necks, then lowered them into the black recesses of spider holes—the spiders would bite the lizards and drag them down. The trick was to pull a spider out of its hole. Then one of us would smash it with a rock. We hated everything that crawled on so many hairy legs. Ants we fried by using a magnifying glass and the power of the sun. We encircled scorpions in a ring of kerosene and set fire to the ring to watch how the insect stung itself in an act of suicide. Once, I slashed the tires of my brand new bike (a bicycle my father had stood in long lines to buy), and I made a double-banded slingshot, the best all the kids in the neighborhood ever saw or held. They envied it, all right. A group of us went out into the back yard to shoot at sparrows. I killed my first as it perched on the clothesline preening its feathers. The pebble shot from my new slingshot broke its breastbone and the bird plummeted to the ground like a rotted mango.

🐢 🐢 🐢

Fueled by the violence of those days, I became an expert at killing. I had learned well from watching my father and uncles slaughter so many animals in our back yard. Pigs, chickens, goats, rabbits, turtles. The pigs, my father knifed in the heart while they ran. "It's the only good way," my father would say, "so they don't squeal." The goats bleated and kicked as they hung by rope from a roof I-beam, their necks about to be slashed. My father would slice through in one swift motion. Their throats opened and so much blood flowed. Then there were the countless chickens and ducks and guinea fowl whose necks my mother wrung. And there were rabbits, turtles, pigeons, turkeys, fish, both from the rivers and the ocean—all killed and gutted before the eyes of so many children.

🐢 🐢 🐢

Stray dogs followed me home from school, mangy, filthy and hungry. My mother wouldn't let me keep any of them as a pet. In those days, as now, people would kill and eat anything in Havana, Cuba. I think she feared the temptation. We raised and kept animals in our yard. So did everyone else in the barrio. Even after severe sanitation laws were passed, people took chances and hid their animals in their bathrooms, bedrooms, closets. One time the military came to our neighborhood and confiscated all the animals. Rounded them up and led them to a huge pit a bulldozer had dug at the corner. All the animals were herded into this pit and set on fire. Ah,

Spared Angola 🐢 125

the carnage and the wail of so many burning animals. On school field trips they took us to the chicken hatcheries and showed us how male chicks were ground to make feed for the zoo animals.

🐢 🐢 🐢

My father, who was a *gusano* then and made to work voluntarily as a killer of horses to feed the lions and tigers at the zoo, never confirmed the story about the baby-chicks -ground-up-as-feed. He did tell us about the monkey which played and teased a cage full of tigers until one day, when it slipped and fell, the tigers quartered it immediately. My father smuggled home some of the horse meat from the horses he killed. And then there were the stories told by the neighborhood punks of sexual perversion with dogs, pigs, goats and even chickens.

🐢 🐢 🐢

My father told me that when he was a kid and his uncle wanted to get him out of a conversation, that he would send my father to *tentar las gallinas*, which meant that my father would have to go into the chicken coop and stick his pinkie into the chickens' cloacas to feel for the next-morning's eggs. I had a bunny which a couple of fierce neighborhood dogs caught and mauled. Cats, too, suffered in our neighborhood. They died regularly in yute sacks hung from trees, beaten up like piñatas. Or they were left in the bags on the railroad tracks.

🐢 🐢 🐢

Virgil Suárez

Such cruelty makes the minds-eye burn, the heart flutter . . . We fished the rivers, roamed the woods for everything and anything edible. Doves, quail, even rats. When my parents sent me off for the summer to San Pablo in the province of Las Villas, to my maternal grandparents, it wasn't any good either— no escape from people and their slaughter of animals. But within the context of a farm, the killing made sense, became less disturbing. I witnessed the castration of pigs and bulls. My grandmother chopped the heads off guinea fowl. Then she'd put me to pluck the feathers and clean each bird. In 1970, the madness stopped when we left for Spain, where the only animals I saw alive were ones people kept as pets. Of course, there were the carcasses at the markets, but people no longer killed and ate their pets—they didn't have to. There I, too, kept my first animals as pets: goldfinches, goldfish, hamsters, a turtle. I kept them throughout my youth in Madrid and, later, when we moved to Los Angeles, California. After so many years I had come to appreciate creatures well kept and alive.

🐢 🐢 🐢

That was a long time ago. These days I have a dog (more on him later) and a garage full of canaries. I've become quite a canaryculturist. During the breeding season, sometimes it becomes necessary, because of genetic disasters, to dispose of a canary chick. Often, if things go wrong, a chick might be born without a limb, or, as was the case recently, without eyes. To have to cull it is to return to the violence I experienced in my youth. But to leave such a creature in pain is unpardonable. So I cull, which means I drown the chick in a glass of water. Recently at a bird show, I asked several bird-keepers what humane methods they utilized. The discussion turned into a heated argument about the best way being

Spared Angola

no good at all, but the majority of us agreed that to kill a bird quickly is to snap its neck.

🐢 🐢 🐢

Now about the dog, our Basset Hound, Sir Mongo of Tallahassee, who, though AKC registered, is far from being a champion specimen. Our dog. Our dog, which has been howling and crying at night since we brought him home as a puppy. His nocturnal whimpering and wheezing is enough to test anyone's patience, and I won't mention his lack of intelligence. Sometimes when he can't stop crying, I get out of bed, naked or clothed, and I walk to the kitchen to plead with him for a little silence, a little rest. But it's no use. He whimpers and cries more. We keep him behind a gate in the kitchen, and when he isn't making noise, he is busy at mischief. He will search and destroy almost everything he can reach, from cereal to fruit to thawing meat to coffee. It's worse when we have visitors. He once stole a friend's pair of glasses and chewed them up, eating glass and plastic. We found only half of the frames. But the nighttime is the worse. There's nothing to do but rage. Once I let myself go and I hit Sir Mongo of Tallahassee with a rolled-up newspaper. He did stop howling, but only briefly enough to catch his breath.

🐢 🐢 🐢

It was during this moment that I caught a glimpse of myself, half-naked, on the window—myself a creature, nocturnal and afraid like any other, driven mad by lack of sleep. When I looked across the dark expanse of the yard, I saw the neighbor's lighted kitchen window. I imagined a person there awake at the same hour, up for a glass of milk, and then, all of a sudden, the same image I saw on my kitchen window: a

Virgil Suárez

man half-naked, rolled-up newspaper in hand, threatening to beat up his dog. No, not easy to explain, the many years as witness and participant in the slaughter and cruelty to animals. What would you think?

After the Accident

for Wasabi who witnessed it

he is all skin & bones,
too thin, his flesh so taut
the veins on his temples welt
ramify all the way down
his face to his eyes, nose, mouth

here sits the same man
who harassed the child,
teenager, & not so long
ago refused to speak
to me because I wore my hair

shoulder length
not good enough for him
who had worn his 50's
Cuban police crew cut,
he listens to exile radio

stations that propagate
crazy notions & ideas
about people he knows next
to nothing about,
nothing to do & all the time

not to get it done
orders & reads
all the junk mail
& catalogues
goes out for walks

Virgil Suárez

around the block, confronts
 total strangers who litter,
helps children cross
the street from the school
at the corner

studies for the naturalization
exam, for he wants
to be a certified
United States citizen
when back in the 60's

when he was being persecuted
for anti-revolutionary
activities, he was a different
man, once threw a makeshift
kerosene lamp against the wall

& set the house on fire,
he was losing his mind
& the government arrested
him & forced him to work
volunteer work

which nearly cost him his life,
this same man who stood
& watched as my mother
(during my days of drink
& staying out all night)

Spared Angola   131

broke my bottles of wine
in the sink & threw
himself on his knees
& braced my legs
when I threatened to leave

the house for good,
the man whom I helped
while he slaughtered
so many animals, the same
who brought dirty movies

in the trunk of the '65 Dodge Dart
to my friend's house
driven by some sense of fatherly
duty to expose me to the flesh,
took me to the shops

then embarrassed me because
he argued with the cashiers
who refused to speak
to him in his native Spanish,
& he knew they spoke it,

but he went ahead & bought
the train set for me, the speed car
set, the bicycle, later the Mustang,
he worked two jobs
because he cared,

Virgil Suárez

though he never admitted it,
more about his family
than most men I know
but the accident changed
all that: 576 pounds

of compressed cardboard
on a pallet fell on him at work,
on my father, the company man,
the lover of eight-to-five jobs,
no questions asked, week in/week out

the weight fell on him & crushed
him, broke his spinal chord
in two places, shattered his skull,
fractured his pelvis into four,
ruptured his testicles, spleen & lower

intestines, took away any semblance
of the man I knew, the man
I know now acts defeated,
has given up, contemplates
the lives that could have been,

speaks of suicide,
of hurling himself from a second story
but the apartment in Hialeah
has bars on the windows,
he knows this is not viable

so he tries to open the passenger
door when I'm driving
but forgets he's buckled
& he cries, curses, shouts
at me, at my mother,

this is not who I was, he screams
this is not who I wanted to be,
my mother caresses his hair
I keep driving & do not look
over at him because I don't

want him to think that I am ashamed
of his behavior
because then he *will* kill himself
I know, so I reach out
& grab his hand

& I tell him what I told him
as he lay unconscious in the ICU,
with so many cables going in/out
of him: that it's okay
he's done good.

how do you tell a man
whose done hard & good
work all his life, he's done
he's done & finished?

Virgil Suárez

Tito the Barber (? - 1995)

I.

who cut my hair
     in Huntington Park,
California in the 70s,
     he was old then
& he still managed
     to hold that straight
razor straight against
     the back of my neck,
told countless stories
     of his youth in some
part of Cuba, when he was young
     like me, then he owned
a suitcase full of money & knew
     women in every town
he went to, gambled at cock
     fights, drank the finest
rum, all this time he's shaving
     & holding steady,
razor against skin.

II.

a decade later when he can't cut
hair anymore because of arthritis
& his nerves being, as he put it,
on edge & poor eyesight,
he takes to strolling the neighborhood, carries a kitchen knife
to be on the safe side, sharp,
tucked between his *camiseta*
& pants, walks unafraid, day-
dreams of those days in the land
long forgotten—but not by him,
no, he walks in back each day,
past the places where the concrete
end & the red dirt & sugar cane
begin, he goes back each day,
dressed in his best, a suitcase
in hand, with somewhere in mind
to go to, things to do, people
to meet, to a life still ahead of him.

Virgil Suárez

Mofongo

for Victor Hernández Cruz

Substance
that can nourish
& bring back the dead.
How often do I crave
this sweet concoction,
this mixing of heavenly
ingredients: *plátano*
verde, chicharrón, manteca,
mojo criollo and *ajo,*
but so difficult to find such
a delicacy in these lonely
highways of gringoland.
The best I've ever tasted
was in the Upper East Side
in a Cuban-Puerto Rican-
Chinese restaurant.
So damn good I had three
servings & left the staff
& patrons in awe
of my hunger & voracity.
This is the sustenance
& so I thought of you,
your beats & rhythms
& how once in a while,
which is most of the time,
when I can't have
this glorious dish,
I turn to you
& nourish myself
with the condiments
& flavors of your
poetry.

Teeth

"I'm a sick man . . . a mean man. There's nothing attractive about me. I think there's something wrong with my liver."

—from *Notes From Underground*
By Fyodor Dostoyevsky

This is all true. It begins with my mother in Habana, Cuba, taking tetracycline during her pregnancy. She didn't know it at the time, but this would have a terrible effect on my teeth, which would forever be stained a yellowish green. It was my name and my teeth which gave me the most trouble during my adolescence. Other kids picked on me, either because of the name or because they said I didn't brush my teeth. Oh, I brushed my teeth. I still do, so hard in fact that I make my gums bleed. Even today, I will not walk away from the bathroom without looking into the mirror and

Virgil Suárez

seeing the trickle of blood rise between the flesh and the tooth enamel. I brush after every meal. I brush when I've had too much coffee. I brush when I think I have bad breath. Growing up in the land of scarcity didn't help any. My mother took me to the dentist in Cuba and they all told her the same. No, even after a lost my milk teeth, the new ones would come out stained. Milk teeth, I've often wondered what that really means? There wasn't any tooth fairy in Havana. When my teeth started loosening up, my relatives showed me how to pull them. It was painless fun. The softening and jiggle one day, and the gap the next. My mother saved all my teeth as I shed them. I never asked what she intended to do with them; and she never offered any clues. I dreamt she'd make pendant earrings out of them. A necklace. A brooch. But my teeth were stained. Ruined for life. Everybody on my mother's side of the family always offered milk. Calcium, they said, calcium was the answer. Nothing helped. I was a sickly child. Who knows how many bottles of Scott's Liver Emulsion I suffered? People kept saying it was my diet. I was sickly and skinny. The dentists told my mother there was nothing to be done. The new teeth came in stained, crooked. I was born in 1962—there'd be no braces for me. The dread and fear of dentists was inflicted upon me early, from so many visits. There was always the faint smell of clove lingering in the air in the waiting rooms. It made the child gag. We sat and waited. My mother would not give up, she'd not have a child with stained and crooked teeth. She took me all over Havana looking for an answer, for the right dentist to save me from a life of ridicule. On those leather chairs I always sank in and braced myself for the worse. The scraping, the picking, and the drilling which came later on. I hated it. I still do. There are statistics that say dentist are among the top professionals to commit suicide. No wonder. Who likes the sons of bitches? Ah, but how I suffered at their hands. When we moved to Madrid, Spain in 1970, the first thing my mother did was take me to a dentist. They, too, confirmed what the Cuban dentists had said. My teeth were stained. It was to be. There, under the enamel, lay the clouds of yellow-green venom. But the diet improved in Spain. I drank milk on a regular basis, and though I hated it, I drank it to please my mother. Cheeses, too. Everything dairy was supposed to have some kind of magical effect on my teeth. But my parents wouldn't give up. In 1974 we arrived in the United States where my parents quickly found work in the factories in Los Angeles, California. They worked hard without insurance of any sort. Still, every year my parents saved enough money for my annual teeth checkup. The dentists who looked into my mouth in the United States all did the same thing, they looked, then stopped and called in their colleagues, come look at this, they'd say. Have you ever seen anything like this—recently? With every visit I started to feel proud, specially when they found cavities because I knew they wanted to get in there and scrape, poke, drill. People who are dentists must have been anteaters in another life, all that digging and rooting. There were a couple of years when my parents didn't have the money. Someone told my father about this retired dentist from Cuba who worked out of his garage. He was cheap. He did good work. The only problem, as I was to find out later, with this dentist was that he didn't use anaesthecia. The first and last time I went over with my father, he drilled my teeth without it. He worked in the garage all right, on an old barber's chair. "Grab the arms real hard," he told me. "When you feel any pain, lift your finger." I looked at my father, who didn't say anything. He knew we needed to go through this. I kept my fingers clawed to the arms of the chair. I tore the leather. The pain sent chills up and down my spine as the drill dug deeper, and the smell of rot came up to my nostrils. This guy had nothing on the dentist in Marathon Man played by Sir Lawrence Olivier. "If I had anaesthecia," the man told my father, "I'd use it. But, I'm not insured for doing this here." My father saw the rage in my stare. I didn't speak to him for weeks. Nothing that was ever tried has worked at getting my teeth straight and clear. Still, not much

Virgil Suárez

improvement was made over the years. I was a teenager by now and rebellion had set in. When my parents spoke of checkups and teeth cleaning, I said no. After much pleading, my mother would take me in to this other Cuban dentist who worked on my teeth and who gave my parents credit. Pay later for the pain today. Great idea, I thought, but this man was and still is the only dentist I've ever trusted. Needless to say, the day he informed my mother he was retiring was the last day I've ever been to the dentist. This was 1983. I was in college. I had found out I didn't have to worry about my teeth. People no longer made a big deal about it. Women liked me or disliked me for other reasons, none of which had anything to do with my teeth. Once in a while they'd come up in friendly conversation. I would say, "Look, look at my teeth," as if to put everything on the table. "Look how stained." It's not that bad, they'd say. And I would tell them the troubles I've had. The last dentist—who I had started to call Christ Dentist (*Cristo El Dentista*) after the beginning of *Miss Lonelyhearts,* a wonderful novel by Nathaneal West—tried a final time to do a new procedure that was guaranteed to mask my kind of problem. It didn't work. It left a couple of off-color spots on my first and second premolars. And somewhere between the dentin and enamel, the stain lingered. I will take my stained teeth to my grave. Since 1983 I have spared myself any more humiliation and pain. The rootcanals so many dentists have promised I'd need. The wisdom teeth came forth and praise be to god, they behaved on their path. I refused braces. No more of those hellish instruments. I know other generations have had it worse. Imagine having a toothache in the wild west, a barber would do the pulling. My friend David Kirby told me once that he read in *Life* that soldiers during World War I sat on a bicycle type of contraption and pedalled fast to motor the drill. Imagine, the faster you pedalled, the better the drill worked. Then came AIDS in 1987 and it's given me a better excuse to tell people when the subject of my teeth comes up. "What are the chances?" they ask. "What are the chances of contracting AIDS from a dentist?" I don't want to find out. There was Kimberly Bergalis who contracted the disease from her dentist. Anyway, since 1983 I have not been to a dentist and neither do I intend to go, which brings me to the epigram of this piece by Dostoyevsky. For the longest time I had not remembered how *Notes From Underground* opened, having read the book a long time ago in college. I always thought that it went something like, *"I'm a sick man . . . a mean man. There's nothing attractive about me. I think there's something wrong with my . . . teeth."* I like that. And I thought I had managed to repress all of my dentist-going experiences when one day I find myself being Lamaze coach to my wife. It's the meeting next to last and the instructor asks us to gather in a circle. There we are, my wife leaning back against me, totally comfortable and relaxed when the instructor asks all the men to relate their most painful (excruciatingly so) moment and it's my turn, and I'm sitting there thinking of all the things that have fucked me up and scarred me, and I think immediately of Dr. Mengele in Los Angeles, the man who worked on my teeth without anaestecia. All the other guys in the Lamaze group look at me as if I'm making this stuff up. Then they see my eyes water. They see the same rage my father saw that afternoon, a rage that, thank heavens, has never reared its ugly head again. My wife didn't know this story. Surely, we had talked about teeth, but I had never told her. Of course, now that we were having our first child, I was worried. I kept thinking about my mother's biggest fear, which is that the stained teeth is in our, mine, genetic pool. Luckily, both my daughters have beautiful straight, clear teeth. Alexandria, the oldest, has gaps between her teeth, which the pediatrician says will be all right. Gabriela has perfect teeth. Soon they will be having their first dentist visit, and I keep thinking of great medical advances in dentistry. For their sake, for mine. For fear that I will have to take them in and that when I smile in the office, the dentist will stop what he or she is doing, look at my mouth, and say "OH, MY GOD, COME EVERYBODY, HAVE A LOOK AT THIS."

Virgil Suárez

The Ways of Guilt

"Guilt is magical."
from "Adultery" a poem by James Dickey

My father calls a day
too late, merely to remind
me that once again
I've forgotten my mother's

birthday, never mind his,
which is a month earlier,
and which I have also
forgotten. He lowers

his voice so that he can
tell me that he will call
my mother and tell her
that I have just called

to wish her a happy
birthday—never mind
that I'm a day too late.
My mother, after he puts

her on, manages to say
that it's all right, all right
for a son to forget a parent's
birthday, but a mother

or father (I'm a father
of two)—and she stops
at "father" to suck
in her breath—should never

forget a son or daughter's
birthday, that would certainly
be unpardonable, like a tiger
eating her cubs. After we

hang up, I think of all those
moments, painfully awkward
and embarrassing when my
parents, left without any other

alternative, reverted to what always
works: guilt. As I hang up
my three-year-old daughter
Alexandria walks into the kitchen

for a glass of cold water. She
looks up at me & must sense
something in the way I look
for she asks, "Daddy, are you

happy?" This is something
she's learned at school,
from hearing her teacher say
bad behavior doesn't make

her happy. This is also the
same child who's asked
in the past where laughter
goes. I look at her & smile

Virgil Suárez

just to reassure her that yes,
I am happy, for the moment,
anyway. Perhaps happiest
to know that when the moment

comes in her own life, I too
will know what buttons to push.
What strings
to pull.

How My Days Go in Suburbia

Everyone gets them, the blues that is,
on Mondays—back to work, back to the grind,
back to the push of the rock uphill,
blues Monday. Tuesday, you get two
of everything, double shots of radio music

or bourbon at the restaurants & bars,
or both, as the system begins to warm up.
Hump day they call Wednesday,
top of the hill, supposedly the most
productive of work days. You can see

where the week's been, where it's headed.
No wonder it's the boss's favorite day.
Thursday has no tag, no label, no name,
other than it's the day next to the last, next
to freedom. It's also, for a younger crowd,

Ladies' Night out, which means another
chance to drink & forget the misery, the grind.
Ah, Friday, you can hear it in the collective sigh
of relief: "Thank God It's Friday!" Everyone
tries to cut work short, clock out early, head

for home, merge, loosen up & get ready for the week
end. You can see them, can't you? the days piling up,
multiplying, day in, day out; week in, week out;
month in, month out; year in, year out.
Get the point. But Friday's come & gone

Virgil Suárez

& the weekend has started with the roar
of the lawn mowers, the lighting of the BBQs,
the jog of the healthy, the mad rush for the sales
& sales & sales—all that shopping to get ready
for the sports on t.v. like monster truck pull

or wrestling (yes, we still believe after all those
punches & kicks, these guys in funny make-up
& costumes, are nothing short of super human).
There's also the get-ready-to-boogie
crowd who look forward to Saturday night,

yes, the weekend is ours & nobody cares
what happens, nobody gives a hoot
what we do with these two days
of supposed rest & relaxation. Unadulterated
fun. We get our sweat suits on & keep them

on all weekend. We settle down & ready to watch
too much t.v. How can we not surrender?
Except some of us are bratty, we don't want
to give in to the spoon-fed methods
the system (it's always *the system* for us

paranoids) utilizes to control, to seduce
us into believing that this is how the rest
of the world lives Monday through Friday,
& of course through the weekend.
Yes, those two days are given names here:

Saturday & Sunday. Even though nobody,
bosses & CEOs included, cares what we do
with our weekends. It's like the two-week vacation
at the end of every year, unless we work them
because, as usual, we are short on cash—

we all know that crunch month's always
around the corner. But, hey, listen, why
wait? Why wait for those walking papers
of retirement at 65 (62 for women)? Why?
It's Sunday night, nothing but bad news,

bad movies on t.v., too many commercials,
bad stomach acid, headaches, pains,
& all the money we worked so hard
for has been spent on cheap thrills
& entertainment. It's the last few hours

of freedom. Why not run outside?
Look up at the full moon & howl.
Take your clothes off & howl up
at the moon like some froth-at-the-mouth
coyote or mad beast out for carnage.

Whatever you do, though, keep in mind the
notion that the neighbors need to get up
early & go off to work & start the routine
all over again, & watch the days go, go by.

Virgil Suárez

The Trouble with Frogs

It's irrational, I know, like the fear of flying
    or high places,
but irresistible nonetheless, for frogs hide
    in the luscious green
of the plantain's fronds. There, they nest
    and call out
for nuptial visitations. Become invisible against
    the corrugated tin
of the outhouse at my grandmother's house,
    then jump. . .
The neighborhood kids catch them and put them
    down my shirt
and in my pants. Who understands the terror
    of this cold and clammy
thing moving against the skin? All the time the child
    thinks there is no return
from such fear. At night beyond the mosquito net,
    they call out.
From Havana to Tallahassee,
    frogs have evolved
into this fear of a childhood not lived,
    not remembered,
but out there, in the distance, they call; they beckon
    no matter how far I travel,
I cannot escape this trouble with frogs.
    All I can do
is embrace the fact that they are there,
    like the past,
calling out; beckoning for the mind to leap.

The Halves

silences gather here
in this new house
for the first time
unbearable

the white noises
audible in the stillness
of the house rebel
against vacancy

yearns to be lived in
& occupied, filled
with human waking
but now in your absence

no comfort even in the hum
of ghosts behind the shut
doors to the empty rooms
but life continues behind

them Alex at her little table
finger-paints or squeezes
clay between her little fingers
delighted with the soft clay

laughter rises & seeps out
under the crevices, her bath-
robe hangs on the hook
next to Del's clothes

where mother & daughter left
them undisturbed they remain
to move them would disrupt
this delicate balance

Virgil Suárez

alone, I bake two loaves
of bread daily, something
to do to pass the time
the sweet aroma brings

shape to the silence
fills the house with more life
forget the blood & skin
amiss here, for there is no

pleasure in loneliness
the birds in the garage
flutter in their cages
while the male canaries

sing to the females
this is the only sound
that I can't control
the only sound to overpower

the silence all day
the mating season
continues into the start
of spring

spring, of course, spring
upon everything, everyone
outside the bulbs break
through the earth

tulips in all the colors
I could find at the home depot
for you, for you
even though you are not here

they will flower soon
perhaps before your return
before your return
I haven't gotten used

to sleeping alone
this is no way to rest
after a day of work
the gaps on the bed

& empty spaces
provide no solace
cannot replace
the warmth of two bodies

I sleep to conjure
rest an impenetrable
silence which should come
only to the dying

okay, I admit it
good or bad or corny
this is nothing more
than a love poem

in the 17 days
of your absence

Virgil Suárez

Brújula/Compass

for David Kirby who named the new directions

I.

North
Havana, Florida
Antiques & rummage
frenzies, a restaurant
that runs out of food
at midday. Nothing
to do but walk & see
the relics of the past

West
Baton Rouge, Tucson,
Los Angeles,
a highway so long
makes the eye water
so much dust & fumes
many lives spent
the next stop
never quite getting there

East
Madrid, Spain
four years of a childhood
in the bitter cold
of a foreign tongue
a happier time
so many lives spend
& the sounds of the bed
springs in parents' room

South
Key West & Havana, Cuba
the ninety-mile stretch
outcasts & exiles
the place of origen
eight years of scars
inflicted upon the child
by time & people: bliss

Spared Angola 🐢 153

II.

we come to the place
where pollen coats
everything; this fertile
earth in the spring:

in the center now,
back in the south end
of America, a fertile time
& what we were spared

we were spared long ago
—Africa so far away,
no longer a possibility
for death & dying

out there in the night,
in the heat that chokes
us out of the house,
so audible & palpable

the American Dream
beckons us,
to be like the insects
swarming in a halo

of a street light,
thank the wind & pay
homage to these new
directions

heed the voices
that have carried
us so far

Virgil Suárez

GLOSSARY

abuela / grandmother

aguardiente / liquor made from the sugar cane

ajo / garlic

alguien / someone; somebody

aquí me quedo / here I stay

balsa / raft

barrio / neighborhood

bohíos / thatched huts

boniatillo / dessert made from sweet potatoes (boniato)

bolero / a type of song

brujería / same as **santería**, a form of African-Cuban
  witchcraft

caca / shit

cabroncito / little bastard

cafecitos / small cups of coffee

calzones / men's boxer shorts, underwear

cámara lenta / slow motion

camiseta / men's undershirt

caracoles / snail shells

carnal / slang for brother

cascabeles / jingle bells

catre / cot

centavos / pennies

Changó / African deity

chicharrón / pork rinds

coco duro / slang for hard-headed

colibrí / hummingbird

compañero / comrade

coño / expletive; expression referring to female genitals, meaning something like shit or damn!

cuando el mar está de cagar, no valen guayabas verdes / expression often used by Cubans to mean "There's no way of preventing bad things from happening."

decímas güajiras / type of Cuban folksong

dulce de coco / dessert made from coconut

Elegua / African deity

empachado / stuffed, sick from overeating

en paz descanse / rest in peace

ese / slang for dude

Fiñe, te vas a romper el coco / kid, you are going to break your head

fuetes / a string, spinner game

güajiro / a Cuban farmer, someone from rural agricultural towns

güarapo / non-alcoholic drink made from the sugar cane

guayo / a percussion instrument

gusano / worm; traitor to the Cuban Revolution who emigrates

hijos de puta / sons of bitches

jarabe / a homemade cough syrup

Virgil Suárez

jicotea / turtle

kimbumbia / a game played with three sticks

la pasamanos / one who heals with his/her hands

la libertad / liberty

la más fina / the finest

la vida / life

la raza / used mainly by Mexican-Americans rooted in Vasconcelos' theory of a cosmic race, which is a synthesis of all races present in the meztizo-a.

la gata de la trece / the cat (female) from 13th Street gang

lagartijas / lizard

Las Siete Potencias / the seven African dieties

leño / same as mota, slang for marijuana

libreta / ration book used in Cuba

locos / madmen

los golpes enseñan / one learns from blows

los Reyes Magos / the three wisemen; the gift of the magi

manteca / lard

mantequilla / butter

maricón / a derogatory term for homosexual

me cago en ti / I shit on you

Maria Caracoles baila el Mozambique / title of popular song in Cuba

me vas a volver loco / you are going to drive me crazy

me oyes? / do you hear me?

melcocha / taffy

mira / look

mochila / military back pack

mojo criollo / a marinade of condiments and spices

mosca / fly

mota / slang for marijuana

muchacho / young man

mucho / a lot, plenty

no te acuerdas de mi? / don't you remember me?

no chingues / don't fuck around

órale / Mexican-American for right now

pachuco / Mexican-American word for gang member

palmeras / palm trees

panocha / Mexican-American word for vagina

papalotes / kites

pasadora de mano / a person who performs a laying of the hands

pendejo / insult; fool, idiot, dupe

pin pan pun / Cuban for spring sprung bed; hard to tell where the "pan" comes from

pinche cabrón / Mexican-American insult

pioneritos / members of Revolutionary youth groups analogous to Boy Scouts

platano verde / green plantain

pomadas / ointments

punto y aparte / period, end of story

rayuela / the game of hopscotch

ruca / Mexican-American word for girlfriend

sabes / you know

sabrosamente / deliciously

sabrosona / delicious; referring to a woman

salsa y sabor / rhythm and flavor

santa / saint (female)

sapos / bullfrogs

siete potencias / African for the Seven Mightily Deities

singada / equivalent of chingada, fucked

socialismo o muerte / Socialism or Death

sonnes / a type of song

suave / smooth

tasita / little cup; demitasse

Virgil Suárez

tentar las gallinas / a certain physical way of checking to
  see if a chicken is due to lay an egg
tía / aunt
tortuguitas / little turtles
trucha / Mexican-American expression for warning
vato / Mexican-American for homeboy; member of same gang
ya vámonos / let's go already
Yemayá / African deity
yerba buena / spearmint
yuca / cassava